MARKET HARBOROUGH TO NEWARK

Vic Mitchell and Keith Smith

MP Middleton Press

Front cover picture: Standing at Leicester Belgrave Road on 7th November 1964 is no. 78028, a BR class 2 2-6-0. It is hauling "The Leicester Railway Society's 25th Anniversary Special". (M.J.Stretton)

Back cover picture: Railway Clearing House map for 1947.

Published March 2016

ISBN 978 1 908174 86 4

© Middleton Press, 2016

Design Deborah Esher
Typesetting Cassandra Morgan

Published by
    Middleton Press
    Easebourne Lane
    Midhurst
    West Sussex
    GU29 9AZ
Tel: 01730 813169
Email: info@middletonpress.co.uk
www.middletonpress.co.uk

Printed in the United Kingdom by Henry Ling Limited, at the Dorset Press, Dorchester, DT1 1HD

CONTENTS

1. Market Harborough to Newark   1-93
2. Leicester Belgrave Road Branch   94-120

ACKNOWLEDGEMENTS

We are very grateful for the assistance received from many of those mentioned in the credits, also from J.Bonsall, A.J.Castledine, G.Croughton, G.Gartside, R.Gilbert, A.C.Hartless, T.Heavyside, F.Hornby, N.Langridge, B.Lewis, S.Hewitt, J.Horne, J.P.McCrickard, R.Owen, Mr D. and Dr. S.Salter, T.Walsh and in particular our always supportive families. Our gratitude also goes to M.Greenwood of the Leicester Transport Heritage Trust.

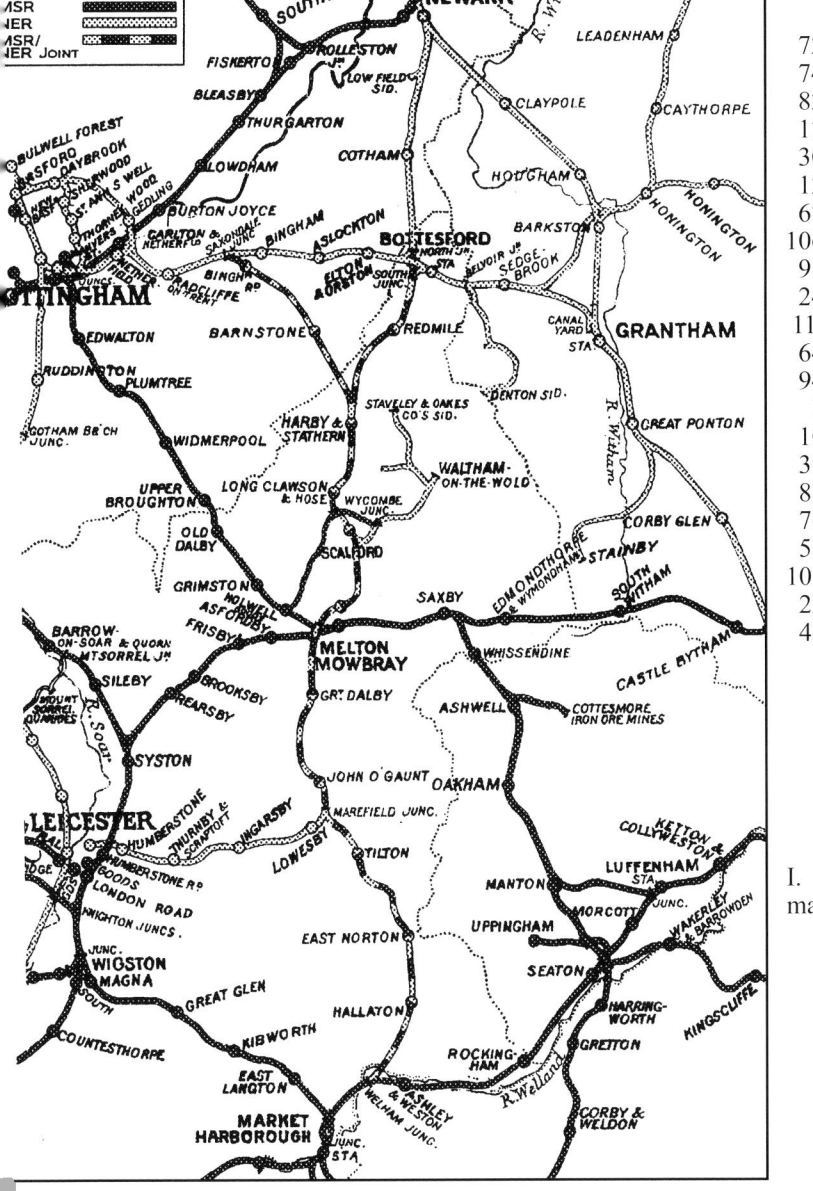

INDEX

72   Barnstone
74   Bingham Road
82   Cotham
17   East Norton
30   Great Dalby
12   Hallaton
67   Harby & Stathern
106 Humberstone
98   Ingarsby
24   John O'Gaunt
111 Leicester Belgrave Road
64   Long Clawson & Hose
94   Lowesby
1   Market Harborough
10   Medbourne
35   Melton Mowbray
88   Newark Northgate
76   Redmile
58   Scalford
101 Thurnby & Scraptoft
22   Tilton
46   Waltham on the Wold

I.   Railway Clearing House map for 1947.

GEOGRAPHICAL SETTING

Our routes traverse mainly limestone, but also red sandstone and other strata. The high ground to the east runs from Dorset, along the Cotswold Hills and north to the Yorkshire Dales, albeit with a gap for the River Humber.

Three rivers rise in the vicinity of Market Harborough: the Avon, which flows southwest, the Soar, which runs northwest and the Welland, which is close to our route initially.

The middle part of our journey is across the Vale of Belvoir, which is largely drained by the River Witham. This reaches The Wash via Lincoln and Boston. Newark had the benefit of the River Trent for commercial navigation for many years. This runs from Nottingham northeast to the River Humber.

Gypsum, cement, limestone and ironstone were amongst the commodities moved away by rail on this line, which was mostly in Leicestershire. The northern eight miles were in Nottinghamshire and south of that, the route ran across the largely level Leicestershire Wolds. The county boundaries are shown with dots on Map I.

The other maps are to the scale of 25ins to 1 mile, with north at the top, unless otherwise indicated.

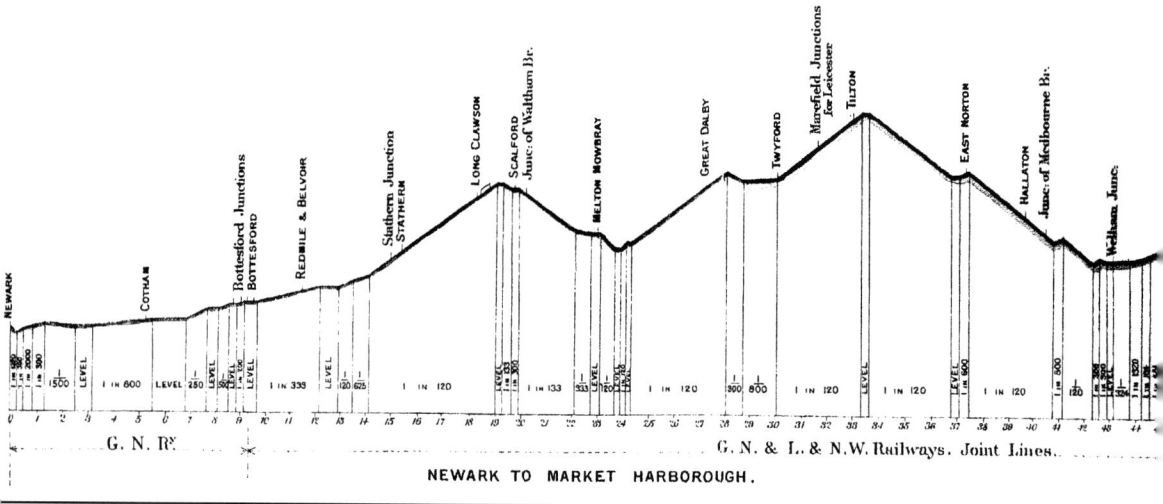

NEWARK TO MARKET HARBOROUGH.

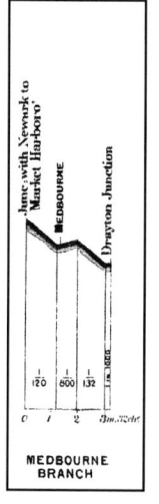

MEDBOURNE
BRANCH

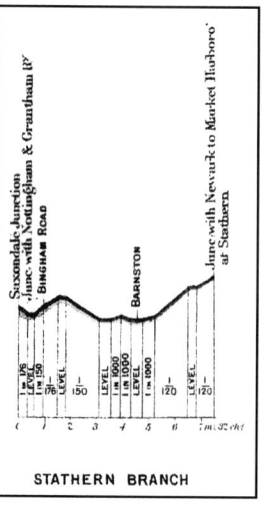

STATHERN BRANCH

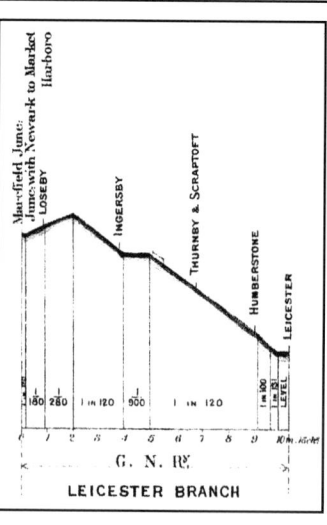

LEICESTER BRANCH

HISTORICAL BACKGROUND

Market Harborough received the London & North Western Railway in 1850, when it opened between Rugby and Rockingham. That company arrived from the south from Northampton in 1859 and the Midland Railway operated from the southeast from Hitchin from 1857. This continued northwest to Leicester that year.

The LNWR and the Great Northern Railway jointly obtained an Act in 1874 to build a line northwards to Newark. It opened in stages in 1878-79: Newark to Bottesford on 1st July 1878, Bottesford to Melton Mowbray on 30th June 1879 and Melton Mowbray south to the LNWR on 15th December 1879. This allowed operation between Market Harborough and Newark to commence.

The route crossed the 1850 Ambergate, Nottingham & Boston & Eastern Junction Railway near Bottesford. It was unusual to have two "ands" in a title.

Newark had received the east-west line of the MR in 1846 and the north-south route of the GNR in 1852.

The branch west to Leicester Belgrave Road was a GNR creation and it came into use on 2nd October 1882, although the terminus did not open until 2nd October of that year. It carried trains to Grantham and Peterborough initially.

The MR became part of the London Midland & Scottish Railway upon the grouping of 1923. The other companies mentioned were constituents of the London & North Eastern Railway. Upon nationalisation in 1948, the LMSR formed much of the London Midland Region, while the latter became the main part of the Eastern Region.

Passenger service was withdrawn from the Belgrave Road branch from 7th December 1953, but some workmens trains continued until 29th April 1957. There were also weekend summer trains to Skegness until 9th September 1962, calling at several stations on the branch. A spur was opened at the west end on 1st June 1964, this allowing most of the branch to be closed.

Services between Market Harborough and Nottingham via Barnstone and to Grantham also ceased on 7th December 1953. Freight withdrawals are given in the captions.

PASSENGER SERVICES

The tables give sample figures for trains running on at least five days per week.

North from Market Harborough

	Weekdays	Sundays
April 1880	5	0
July 1910	5	0
September 1925	5	0
June 1952	4	0

Trains stopped at most stations on their journeys to Nottingham or Grantham. Newark was the destination for several trains in the early years, but this diminished to zero by about 1939.

East from Leicester

The table below excludes expresses, which varied seasonally to serve the holiday traffic, until 1962. Examples are shown in the timetable samples and in the captions.

	Weekdays	Sundays
June 1883	5	0
March 1909	8	0
October 1923	6	0
June 1951	3	0
August 1957	0	1

Before World War I there were about 12 trains in each direction between John O'Gaunt and Harby & Stathern. Half of them worked between Grantham and Leicester and half between Northampton and Nottingham, with three passenger trains each way daily between Leicester Belgrave Road and Peterborough North, via the Lowesby, Medbourne and Longville curves, but this latter service was discontinued in 1916.

BLISWORTH, NORTHAMPTON, MARKET HARBRO', MELTON MOWBRAY, NOTTINGHAM, NEWARK, RUGBY and STAMFORD.—London and North Western.

Down.	mrn	mrn	mrn	mrn	non	non	aft	aft	aft
140 London (Euston) dp	....	5 15	7 30	1010	12 0	12 0	3b0	....	6 0
Blisworth Junction dep	Wednesdays only.	....	9 10	1155	1 45	....	4 50	....	8 10
Northmptn (Castle Sta.,		7 30	9 20	12 5	1 55	3 15	5 0	4 50	8 20
Brampton . . [Black Lion		7 39	9 29	1216	2 4	d	5 11	5 1	8 31
Spratton .... [Hill)		7 45	9 35	1222	2 10	d	5 18	5 8	8 37
Brixworth		7 48	9 38	1225	2 13	d	5 21	5 11	8 40
Lamport		7 54	9 44	1231	2 19	d	5 27	5 17	8 46
Kelmarsh		8 2	9 52	1239	2 27	d	5 34		8 53
Clipstone & Oxendn [205		8 5	9 55	1242	2 30	d	5 39		8 58
Market Harbro' 200, a		8 15	10 3	1252	2 39	3 42	5 47		9 8
L. & N. W. and G. N. Joint.									
Market Harbro' dep		8 17	1010	1 25	....	3 44	5 55		Stop
Hallaton		8 30	1023	1 38	....	3 56	6 8		....
East Norton		8 36	1028	1 44	....	4 1	6 14		....
Tilton		8 44	1035	1 52	....	4 8	6 22	Saturdays only.	....
Burrow and Twyford		8 52	1042	2 0	....	4 15	6 30		....
Great Dalby		8 59	1048	2 7	....	4 22	6 37		....
Melton Mowbry 218	7 15	9 8	1057	2 16	....	4 31	6 46		....
Scalford	7 26	9 14	11 3	2 23	....	4 37	6 53		....
Long Clawson	7 36	9 20	11 7	2 29	....	4 42	6 59		....
Harby & Stathern a	7 43	9 26	1113	2 34	....	4 47	7 4		....
Harby & Stathern d	7 46	9 28	1114	2 36	....	....	7 6	....	....
Barnstone	7 57	9 36	1122	2 44	....	....	7 14	....	....
Bingham Road	8 7	9 44	1130	2 52	....	....	7 22	....	....
Radcliffe 119	8 15	9 52	1138	3 0	....	....	7 30	....	....
Colwick Junc. 119	8 22	9 59	1144	3 6	....	....	7 36	....	....
Nottingham ....arr	8 30	10 5	1150	3 12	....	....	7 42	....	....
Harby & Stathern d	Stop	9 53	1116	4 25	....	4 48	7 8	....	....
Red Mile, for Belvoir		10 0	1123	4 32	....	4 54	7 15	....	....
Bottesford (New Sta.)		10 5	1127	4 37	....	4 58	7 20	....	....
Cotham .... [199, 213		1014	1135	4 47	....	....	7 29	....	....
Newark 128, 131, arr		1025	1144	4 59	....	5 15	7 40	....	....
Retford 128 arr	Mondays only.	1135	1227	....	....	5 45	8 9	aft	aft
Rugby Line.									
140 London (Eus.) dp		....	7 30	1010	2 45		3 0	5 5	6 0
Rugby Junction dep		8 30	1050	1220	4 55		5 20	7 10	8 40
Clifton Mill		8 34	....	a	....		a	a	a
Lilbourne		8 40	....	1230	....		5 30	7 20	8 50
Yelvertoft		8 46	....	1236	....		5 36	7 26	8 56
Welford & Kilworth 1		8 55	11 5	1245	....	1, Station for Lutterworth.	5 45	7 35	9 5
Theddingworth		9 3	....	a	....		5 53	7 43	9 12
Lubenham		9 9	....	1257	....		5 59	7 49	9 19
Market Harbro' 200		9 15	1122	1 8	5 21		6 5	7 55	9 25
Market Harbro' ..dep	5 10	9 17	1124	1 5	5 22		6 10	7 57	....
Ashley and Weston	5 35	9 28	1135	1 16	....		6 21	8 8	....
Rockingham	6 15	9 40	1146	1 28	....		6 33	8 20	....
Seaton and Uppingham	6 30	9 49	1154	1 37	5 57		6 42	8 31	....
Luffenham 218	7 25	10 5	1210	1 50	6 6		6 54	8 45	....
Stamford 128, 131 arr	7 40	1020	1220	2 5	6 20		7 8	8 57	....

From Peterboro', see p[illegible]		mrn	mrn	mrn	mrn	mrn	aft	aft	aft
Stamford .... dep		7b0	9 0	....	1030	1230		2 25	6 30
Luffenham		7 12	9 12	....	1042	1242		2 37	6 42
Seaton and Uppingham		7 22	9 25	....	1055	1252		2 50	6 55
Rockingham		7 35	9 41	....	....	....		3 7	7 4
Ashley & Weston . [205		7 47	9 51	....	....	....		3 18	7 14
Market Harbro' 200, a		8 1	10 2	....	1130	1 19		3 31	7 25
Rugby Line.									
Market Harbro'	7 15	8 25	10 7	...	1132	1 21	d Stops to take up for Stations North of Market Harbro'. e Stops to set down from Stations North of Market Harbro'.	3 35	7 26
Lubenham	7 21	8 31	1012	....	....	....		3 41	7 31
Theddingworth .	7 28	8 37	....	....	....	....		3 48	a
Wlfrd & Kilwth 1	7 40	8 45	1027	....	1148	....		3 57	7 42
Yelvertoft	7 49	8 54	....	....	....	....		4 5	7 50
Lilbourne . . [215	7 59	9 0	....	....	a	....		4 10	7 56
Clifton Mill [156	8 10	a	....	....	....	....		4 18	....
Rugby 145, 140,	8 15	9 10	1040	....	12 5	1 50		4 25	8 5
145 London (Eus.)	1030	1230	1250	....		....		6 45	1020
L. & N. W. and G. N. Joint.									
Retford 131 dep		....	7 15	8 35		9 49		2 31	4 51
Newark .... dep		....	7 50	9 25	a Stop when required. b Through carriages between London and Stamford.	1035		3 30	6 10
Cotham		....	8 1	....		1046		3 42	6 20
Bottesford (New Sta.)		....	8 11	9 40		1055		3 52	6 29
Red Mile, for Belvoir		....	8 16	9 45		11 0		3 57	6 34
Harby & Stathern a		....	8 24	9 52		11 7		4 5	6 40
Nottingham ..dep		....	8 10	....		1115		3 45	6 15
Colwick Junction .		....	8 16	....		1121		3 51	6 21
Radcliffe		....	8 20	....		1125		3 55	6 25
Bingham Road		....	8 28	....		1132		4 3	6 33
Barnstone		....	8 36	....		1140		4 11	6 39
Harby & Stathern a		....	8 44	....		1147		4 19	6 46
Harby & Stathern d		....	8 46	9 54		1149		4 21	6 47
Long Clawson		....	8 53	10 1		1154		4 28	6 57
Scalford		....	8 58	10 6		1159		4 33	6 59
Melton Mowbry 218		....	9 7	1015		12 8		4 42	7 6
Great Dalby		....	9 15	1024		1216		4 50	7 13
Burrow and Twyford		....	9 23	1032		1224		4 58	7 20
Tilton		....	9 31	1040		1232		5 6	7 27
East Norton		....	9 39	1048		1240		5 14	7 35
Hallaton . . [200, 205		....	9 45	1054		1246		5 21	7 41
Market Harbro'. arr		....	9 53	11 7		1 0		5 35	7 54
Market Harbro' ..dep		8 3	10 8	1112		1 25	3 40	6 12	8 0
Clipstone and Oxenden		8 9	1014	e		1 31	3 48	6 18	....
Kelmarsh		8 12	1018	e		1 34	3 51	6 22	8 7
Lamport		8 22	1028	e		1 44	3 59	6 33	8 17
Brixworth		8 27	1034	e		1 49	4 5	6 39	....
Spratton		8 30	1037	e		1 52	4 8	6 42	8 25
Brampton .... [212		8 37	1044	e		1 59	4 14	6 49	8 32
N'thamptn (Castle Sta.)		8 45	1058	1142		2 10	4 24	6 58	8 40
Blisworth J. 145, 140 a		8 55	11 5	....		....	4 34	7 10	8 50
145 London (Euston) arr		1110	1250	....		5 30	7 10	....	1035

April 1880

July 1910

NEWARK, MELTON MOWBRAY, LEICESTER, and NORTHAMPTON.—Great Northern and London and North Western.

Miles		Up.	Week Days.																						Sn
			mrn	mrn	mrn	mrn	mrn	mrn	mrn	mrn	mrn	aft	aft	aft	aft	aft	aft	aft	aft	aft	aft	aft	aft	aft	aft	aft
		Newark .... dep.	....	....	5b28	....	8b10	....	Mondays, Wednesdays, and Saturdays.	b	1034	....	....	....	....	3 12	3 48	....	5b12	....	....	....	....	7b19	....	....
5¼		Cotham	....	....	....	....	....	....		....	....	....	....	....	....	3 20	Through Express, Scarboro' and Bridlington to Leicester.	....	....	....	....	....	....	....	....	....
11½		Redmile, for Belvoir ..	....	....	....	....	....	....		....	....	....	....	....	....	3 32		....	....	....	....	....	....	....	....	....
15½		Harby & Stathern arr.	....	....	....	....	....	....		....	....	....	....	....	....	3 40		....	....	....	....	....	....	....	....	....
—	Mls	Grantham .... dep.	....	....	7 30	....	9 5	....		....	11 5	1245	....	....	....	3 5		....	5 58	....	....	....	....	7 50	....	....
—	4½	Sedgebrook	....	....	a	....	....	....		....	a	1252	....	....	....	3 12		....	j	....	....	....	....	7 57	....	....
—	7¼	Bottesford	....	....	7 41	....	9 16	....		....	1116	1259	....	....	....	3 19		....	6 9	....	6 37	....	....	8 4	8 34	7 58
—	11¼	Redmile, for Belvoir	....	....	7 47	....	9 23	....		....	1122	1 6	....	....	....	3 26		....	6 16	....		....	....	8 11	....	....
—	15¼	Harby & Stathern	....	....	7 54	....	9 29	....		....	1128	1 12	....	....	....	3 32		....	6 22	....		....	....	8 17	....	....
—	Mls	Nottingham* dep.	....	....	....	8 0	9 0	Tuesdays only.		1050	....	....	....	....	2 30	....		4 0	....	6 0	Fridays and Saturdays.	....	....	....	....	....
—	2½	Netherfield	....	....	....	8 6	9 6			1056	....	....	....	....	2 37	....		....	....	6 6		....	....	....	....	....
—	4¾	Radcliffe-on-Trent arr.	....	....	....	....	9 10			f	....	....	....	....	2 43	....		....	....	....		....	....	....	....	....
—		Radcliffe-on-Trent dep.	....	....	....	....	9 11			....	....	....	....	....	2 44	....		....	....	f		....	....	....	....	....
—	8	Bingham Road † ..	....	....	....	8 16	9 18			11 6	....	....	....	....	2 51	....		....	....	6 17		....	....	....	....	....
—	11½	Barnstone	....	....	....	8 23	9 25			1113	....	....	....	....	2 58	....		h	....	6 25		....	....	....	....	....
—	15	Harby & Stathern	....	....	....	8 30	9 32			1121	....	....	....	....	3 5	....		4 24	....	6 31		....	....	....	....	....
—		Harby & Stathern dep.	....	....	7 55	8 32	9 34	9 41	9 41	1131	1136	1 13	....	Saturdays only.	3 7	3 44		4 25	6 25	6 35		....	....	8 19	....	....
18¼		Long Clawson and Hose	....	....	8 1	8 39	....	9 47	9 47	....	1142	1 19	....		3 14	3 50		....	6 31	6 43		....	....	8 26	....	....
20		Scalford	....	....	8 6	8 43	n	9 51	9 51	• i	1146	1 23	....		3 18	3 55		....	6 35	6 48		....	....	8 31	....	....
23¼		Melton Mowbray 591, 592, 593 arr	....	....	8 12	8 49	9 47	9 57	9 57	1144	1152	1 29	....		3 25	4 1	4 19	4 37	6 41	6 54	7 3	....	....	8 37	8 56	8 20
		Melton Mowbray 591, 592, 593 dep	....	....	8 15	8 53	9 51	....	9 59	1146	1154	1 31	....		3 28	4 5	4 27	4 41	6 43	6 58	7 6	....	....	8 40	8 58	8 22
27		Great Dalby	....	....	8 22	9 0	b	....	10 6	....	12 1	1 38	....		3 35	4 12	....	b	6 50	7 5	....	....	....	8 47	....	....
30¼		John O'Gaunt	....	....	8 29	9 7	10 3	....	1013	1159	12 8	1 45	....		3 43	4 19	....	4 51	6 57	7 13	....	....	....	8 54	....	....
32½		Tilton	....	....	....	9 14	c	....	....	12 7	....	....	....		3 50	....	....	....	....	7 20	....	7k30	....	....	....	....
32¼		Loseby	....	7 52	8 34	....	....	....	1018	....	1213	1 50	....	2 50	....	4 24	....	....	7 2	....	....	7 36	....	9 0	....	....
35		Ingersby ††	....	7 58	8 40	....	....	....	1026	....	1219	1 56	....	2 56	....	4 30	....	....	7 8	....	....	7 42	....	9 6	....	....
38¼		Thurnby & Scraptoft	....	8 4	8 46	....	....	....	1032	....	1225	2 2	....	3 2	....	4 36	....	....	7 13	....	....	7 48	....	9 12	....	....
40¼		Humberstone ‡‡	....	8 10	8 51	....	....	....	1038	....	1231	2 8	....	3 8	....	4 42	g	....	7 20	....	7 31	7 54	....	9 18	9 28	8 50
41½		Leicester ‡ 592 .. arr.	....	8 15	8 55	....	....	....	1043	....	1236	2 15	....	3 13	....	4 47	4 58	....	7 25	....	7 35	7 59	....	9 23	9 32	8 54
37½		East Norton	....	....	....	9 21	1016	....	....	1215	....	....	....	....	3 58	....	....	....	....	7 28	....	....	....	....	Through Express from Skegness, see page 387.	Thro' from Mablethorpe & Skegness, see page 387.
39¾		Hallaton 388	....	....	....	9 27	b	....	....	1221	....	....	....	....	4 4	....	....	b	....	7 34	....	....	....	....		
46½		Market Harboro' 443, 549 arr.	....	....	....	9 37	1031	....	....	1231	....	....	....	....	4 14	....	....	5 15	....	7 44	....	....	....	....		
		Market Harboro' 443, 549 dep.	7 45	....	....	9 47	1033	....	....	1239	....	....	3 0	....	4 16	....	....	5 17	....	7 48	....	....	7 53	....		
50		Clipston and Oxendon ..	7 53	....	....	9 55	....	....	....	1247	....	....	....	....	4 25	....	....	....	....	....	....	....	8 1	....		
51¼		Kelmarsh	7 56	....	....	9 58	b	....	....	1250	....	....	b	....	4 29	....	....	....	....	....	....	....	8 4	....		
55		Lamport	8 3	....	....	10 5	b	....	....	1258	....	....	b	....	4 37	....	....	....	....	....	....	....	8 12	....		
57		Brixworth	8 8	....	....	1010	b	....	....	1 4	....	....	3 16	....	4 43	....	....	5 33	....	....	....	....	8 18	....		
58		Spratton	8 11	....	....	1013	....	....	....	1 8	....	....	....	....	4 47	....	....	....	....	....	....	....	8 22	....		
60¼		Pitsford and Brampton	8 21	....	....	1019	....	....	....	1 14	....	....	....	....	4 53	....	....	r	....	....	....	....	8 28	....		
64¾		Northmpton § 413 arr.	8 29	....	....	1027	11 0	....	....	1 29	....	....	3 28	....	5 1	....	....	5 45	....	8 12	....	....	8 35	....		
130¾		413 London (Euston) arr	1010	....	....	....	1235	....	....	4 5	....	....	5 15	....	....	....	....	7 40	....	1125	....	....	1125	....		

NOTES.

- **a** Stop when required to take up for Harby and beyond.
- **b** Take up for London on giving notice at Station.
- *b* Via Grantham.
- **c** Stops at 10 9 mrn. to take up for Northampton and beyond.
- **f** Takes up when required.
- **g** Sets down when required from Newark and beyond.
- **h** Sets down when required, or takes up for Market Harboro' and beyond.
- **i** Takes up for Tilton & beyond on giving notice at Station.
- **j** Stops when required to take up for Redmile and beyond.
- *k* Wednesdays and Saturdays.
- **n** Stops on Thursdays and Fridays to set down from Nottingham and beyond on informing Guard.
- **r** Stops to set down from John O'Gaunt and beyond on notice being given to the Guard at the preceding *stopping* Sta.
- *t* Leaves at 8 8 mrn. on Mons.
- • London Road (Low Level).
- † About ¾ mile to Bingham (G.N.) Station.
- ‡ Belgrave Rd. § Castle Sta.
- †† Station for Houghton-on-the-Hill (1½ miles).
- ‡‡ ¾ mile to Humberstone Road Station (Midland).

GRANTHAM, NOTTINGHAM, LEICESTER, and MARKET HARBORO'.—L. & N. E. and L. M. & S.

Miles.	Up.	Week Days only. mrn	ngt	mrn	mrn	mrn		mrn	mrn		aft	aft		aft	aft		aft	aft		
	688 London (King's Cross)..dep.	....	1045	4 45	....	5 5	....	7 15	10 10	....	....	1 15	....	1 40	....	....	4 0	....	....	....
	736 Mablethorpe .... "	....	....	....	....	7g10	....	....	9 25	....	....	12 5	....	12h5	....	....	....	....	....	....
	736 Sutton-on-Sea .... "	....	....	....	....	7g17	....	....	9 33	....	....	1212	....	12h12	....	....	....	....	....	....
	736 Skegness .... "	....	....	....	....	6a35	....	....	9 30	....	....	12 5	....	12h50	....	....	....	....	....	....
	736 Boston .... "	....	....	....	....	7a40	....	....	11 0	....	....	1 10	....	1v45	....	....	....	....	....	....
	695 Newark .... "	....	mrn	....	....	7 50	....	9 3	12 32	....	12 54	....	....	3 31	....	....	5 46	....	....	....
—	Grantham .... dep.	....	5d5	7 30	....	9 5	....	9d48	12 55	....	1d28	3 25	....	5d45	....	....	6 55		....	....
4½	Sedgebrook	....	....	....	....	9 13	....	....	1 3	....	1d36	3 33	....	5d53	....	....	....		....	....
7¼	Bottesford	....	....	7 41	....	9 20	....	....	1 12	....	1d43	3 39	....	6d0	....	....	7 7		....	....
11¾	Redmile, for Belvoir	....	....	7 48	....	9 27	....	....	1 19	....	....	3 47	....	....	....	....	7 14		....	....
15½	Harby and Stathern ..... arr.	....	....	7 55	....	9 34	....	....	1 25	....	....	3 54	....	....	....	....	7 21		....	....
—	Mls Nottingham A .... dep.	....	6 50	....	8 50	....	....	1030	....	....	2 50	....	....	6 25	....	....	....	Saturdays only.	....	....
—	2½ Netherfield & Colwick arr.	....	6 55	....	8 55	....	....	1035	....	....	2 55	....	....	6 30	....	....	....		....	....
	Netherfield & Colwick dep.	....	6 56	....	8 56	....	....	1036	....	....	2 56	....	....	6 31	....	....	....		....	....
—	4¾ Radcliffe-on-Trent	....	7 1	....	9 0	....	....	1041	....	....	3 1	....	....	6 36	....	....	....		....	....
—	8 Bingham Road B	....	7 8	....	9 8	....	....	1048	....	....	3 8	....	....	6 43	....	....	....		....	....
—	11½ Barnstone	....	7 18	....	9 15	....	....	1055	....	....	3 15	....	....	6 50	....	....	....		....	....
—	15 Harby and Stathern . arr.	....	7 26	....	9 23	....	....	11 3	....	....	3 23	....	....	6 57	....	....	....		....	....
—	Harby and Stathern ...... dep.	....	7 29	7 59	9 38	9 44	....	11 5	1 30	....	3 26	3 59	....	6 59	....	....	7 24		....	....
18½	Long Clawson and Hose	....	7 36	8 6	....	9 50	....	1111	1 36	....	3 32	4 6	....	7 5	....	....	7 30		....	....
20	Scalford	....	7 41	8 12	Aa	9 55	....	1116	1 42	....	3 37	4 13	....	7 9	....	....	7 35		....	....
23½	Melton Mowbray 590, 592, 593 arr.	....	7 48	8 18	9 51	10 2	....	1122	1 48	....	3 43	4 19	....	7 15	....	....	7 42		....	....
	Melton Mowbray dep.	....	7 52	8 25	9 54	10 17	....	1125	1 51	....	3 46	4 24	....	7 17	....	....	7 44	9 25	....	....
27	Great Dalby	....	7 59	8 32	Bb	10 24	....	1132	1 58	....	3 53	4 31	....	7 26	....	....	7 51	9 32	....	....
30½	John O'Gaunt .... arr.	....	8 5	8 38	10 5	10 30	....	1138	2 5	....	3 59	4 37	....	7 32	....	....	7 57	9 38	....	....
—	John O'Gaunt .... dep.	7 55	....	8 40	....	10 40	....	....	2 8	....	....	4 40	....	....	....	....	8 0	9 39	....	....
32½	Lowesby	8 0	....	8 45	....	10 45	....	....	2 13	....	....	4 45	....	....	7 30	....	8 5	9 45	....	....
35	Ingersby C	8 6	....	8 52	....	10 52	....	....	2 20	....	....	4 52	....	....	7 36	....	8 12	9 52	....	....
38½	Thurnby and Scraptoft	8 12	....	8 58	....	10 59	....	....	2 26	....	....	4 58	....	....	7 42	....	8 19	9 58	....	....
40½	Humberstone D ...... [796	8 18	....	9 3	....	11 5	....	....	2 31	....	....	5 3	....	....	7 49	....	8 25	10 3	....	....
41½	Leicester F 367, 598, arr.	8 25	....	9 8	....	11 10	....	....	2 36	....	....	5 8	....	....	7 53	....	8 30	10 8	....	....
—	John O'Gaunt .... dep.	....	8 8	....	10 6	....	....	1141	....	....	4 2	....	....	7 33	....	....	....	....	....	....
32¾	Tilton	....	8 15	....	Bb	....	....	1148	....	....	4 10	....	....	7 40	....	....	....	....	....	....
37¼	East Norton	....	8 25	....	1020	....	....	1158	....	....	4 18	....	....	7 48	....	....	....	....	....	....
39¾	Hallaton .... [547	....	8 33	....	Cc	....	....	12 3	....	....	4 24	....	....	7 54	....	....	....	....	....	....
46½	Market Harboro' 363, 364, arr	....	8 45	....	1037	....	....	1215	....	....	4 37	....	....	8 5	....	....	....	....	....	....
64¼	363 Northampton (Castle) . arr.	....	10 7	....	1113	....	....	1 25	....	....	5 23	....	....	8 48	....	....	....	....	....	....
130¼	363 London (Euston) ...... "	....	12 0	....	1240	....	....	4 15	....	....	7 20	....	....	11 35	....	....	....	....	....	....

A London Road (Low Level).
Aa Stops to take up for beyond Market Harboro' and to set down from Nottingham.
a Departs Skegness at 7 25 and Boston at 8 12 mrn. on Mondays. Via Bottesford.
B Over ¾ mile to Bingham Station.
Bb Stops to take up for beyond Northampton.
C Station for Houghton-on-the-Hill (1½ miles).
Cc Calls regularly on Tuesdays; on other days stops to take up for beyond Northampton.
D ¾ mile to Humberstone Road Station.
d Via Radcliffe-on-Trent.
F Belgrave Road.
g Mondays only, via Bottesford.
h Via Peterboro' (North). On Wednesdays, via Sleaford.
v Via Peterboro' (North). On Wednesdays departs Boston 2 45 aft. via Sleaford.

September 1925

June 1952

Table 75 GRANTHAM, NOTTINGHAM, NORTHAMPTON and LEICESTER

Miles from Nottingham (Vic.)	Miles from Grantham		Week Days only a.m	p.m	a.m	a.m	a.m.	p.m	p.m	a.m.	p.m	p.m	p.m.		p.m.	
		1 LONDON (King's C.) dep	..	11V45	..	..	3 50	Saturdays only	..	11C20	..	..	12n45	..	2L18	..
		1 PETERBOROUGH (N.). "	..	1aA22	..	..	7 40		..	12p21	..	..	..	..	3 52	..
		68 GRIMSBY TOWN ..... "	..	..	..	..	..		..	10D0	..	..	..	..	2U42	..
		67 MABLETHORPE ...... "	..	..	..	..	..		..	9 28	12 14	..	1 50	..	11‡29	..
		67 SUTTON-ON-SEA ..... "	..	..	..	..	..		..	9 36	12 22	..	1 58	..	11‡20	..
		67 SKEGNESS .... "	..	..	..	..	..		..	9 30	1 45	..	..	..	1N4	..
		67 BOSTON .... "	..	..	..	..	..		..	11 25	2 24	..	2 46	..	1E47	..
		77 LINCOLN (Central) .. "	..	..	..	..	7 28		..	12 50	..	..	2 3	..	4X45	..
				p.m			p.m.			a.m.			a.m.		a.m	..
		1 EDINBURGH (Wav.).. dep	..	8B0	..	..	11F30	TC (until 6th September incl.) Leicester (L.R.) dep. 12 35 pm to Brighton, Eastbourne, and Hastings, pages 640 and 230	..	..	Saturdays only	..	..	—	10P0	..
		1 NEWCASTLE .... "	..	11B25	..	..	2a44		..	10 0		..	10 15	..	12pP36	..
		1 YORK .... "	..	1a26	..	..	4 44		..	11 41		..	12 5	..	12P5	..
		1 HULL .... "	..	9pV15	..	..	..		..	10 50		..	12t0	..	1Z30	..
		1 BRADFORD (Exch.).. "	..	9V40	..	..	..		..	10 53		..	11 45	..	1b40	..
		1 LEEDS (Central).... "	..	10V35	..	..	1 50		..	11 20		..	12 8	..	2b0	..
		1 DONCASTER .... "	..	2a17	..	..	5 37		..	12 24		..	1t14	..	2c50	..
		1 RETFORD .... "	..	..	..	..	6 8		..	12 55		..	12 54	..	3d16	..
			a.m	a.m.	a.m	a.m	a.m.		p.m	p.m.		p.m	p.m.		p.m.	..
	—	Grantham .... dep	..	4K55	..	..	8K48		..	2 0	TC Skegness to Leicester (Belgrave Road)	..	3T0	..	5K30	..
	4½	Sedgebrook	..	..	..	..	8K56		..			..	3T8	..	5K38	..
	7¼	Bottesford	..	5K6	..	..	9K2		..			..	3R51	..	5K44	..
	10¾	Redmile	..	..	..	..	..		..			..	..	..	..	..
	14½	Harby and Stathern.. arr	..	..	..	..	..		..			..	..	..	..	..
—	—	Nottingham (Vic) ... dep	..	6 10	..	..	10 47		..	Saturdays only		..	Saturdays only	..	6 34	..
¾	—	(L.Rd. H.L.) "	..	6 14	..	..	10 50		..			..		..	6 37	..
3½	—	Netherfield and Colwick..	..	6R23	..	..	10 56		..			..		..	6 43	..
5½	—	Radcliffe-on-Trent	..	6 29	..	..	11 1		..			..		..	6 48	..
12¼	—	Barnstone	..	6 40	..	..	11 12		..			..		..	6 59	..
15¾	—	Harby and Stathern arr	..	6 47	..	..	11 19		..			..		..	7 6	..
—	—	Harby and Stathern.. dep	..	6 49	..	..	11 20		..			..		..	7 9	..
18½	17	Long Clawson and Hose....	..	6 55	..	..	11 26		..			..		..	7 15	..
20¼	18¾	Scalford	..	7 0	..	..	11 30		..			..		..	7 20	..
23½	22	Melton Mowbray ... arr	..	7 6	..	..	11 36		..	2 34	3 50	..	4 17	..	7 26	..
		Melton Mowbray ... dep	..	7 10	7 35	..	11 39		1 55	2 35	3 54	4 0	4 21	..	7 28	..
27¼	25¾	Great Dalby	..	7 17	7 42	..	11 46		2 2	..	..	4 7		..	7 35	..
30½	29	John o'Gaunt .... arr	..	7 21	7 47	..	11 52		2 7	..	..	4 12		..	7 41	..
—	—	John o'Gaunt ..... dep	..	7 22	..	..	11 54			..	..	4 13	TC Mablethorpe and Sutton-on-Sea to Leicester (Bel. Rd.)	..	7 42	..
33½	—	Tilton	..	7 29	..	..	12 1		Saturdays only	..	..	4 25		..	7 49	..
37½	—	East Norton	..	7 36	..	..	12 8			..	..	4 32		..	7 57	..
40	—	Hallaton	..	7 42	..	..	12 14			..	..	4 37		..	8 4	..
46¾	—	Market Harborough arr	..	7 54	..	..	12 26			..	..	4 49		..	8 23	..
		Market Harborough dep	7 38	..	..	9 20	12 32	1 7		..	..	5 0		..	8 29	..
50¼	—	Page 469a Clipston and Oxendon	7 45	..	..	9 27	12 39	..		..	..	5 7		..	8 36	..
51½	—	Page 469a Kelmarsh	..	..	..	..	12 42	..		..	..	5 10		..	8 39	..
55¼	—	Page 469a Lamport	7 53	..	..	9 34	12 48	..		..	..	5 16		..	8 45	..
57½	—	Page 469a Brixworth	7 59	..	..	9 38	12 52	..	..	..	..	5 20		..	8 49	..
64¾	—	Page 469a Northampton (C.).. arr	8 10	..	..	9 49	1 5	1 43	..	..	..	5 31		..	9 9	..
—	—	John o'Gaunt .... dep	..	..	7 50	..	..	Sats. only	2 8	..	..	..		—	..	..
—	31	Lowesby	..	..	7 55	..	..		2 13	2 52	..	..		—	..	..
—	34	Ingarsby for Houghton.....	..	..	8 1	..	..		2 19	2 58	..	..		—	..	..
—	36¾	Thurnby and Scraptoft.....	..	..	8 7	..	..		2 25	3 4	4J21	..		—	..	..
—	39	Humberstone	..	..	8 12	..	..		2 30	3 9	4R30	..	4R52	—	..	..
—	40½	Leicester (Belgrave Rd.) arr	..	..	8 17	..	..		2 35	3 14	4 35	..	4 57	..	..	..

NOTES

A Dep. 1 34 a.m on Mondays
a a.m.
B Except Saturday nights. Dep. Edinburgh 10 0 p.m. and Newcastle 12 41 ngt. on Mondays, Fridays. and Sundays
b On Fridays, also on Saturdays 12th July to 6th September inclusive dep. Bradford 2 0 and Leeds 2 20 p.m.
C Dep. 10 35 a.m. on 13th September
c Dep. 3 58 p.m. on Fridays. On Saturdays 12th July to 6th September inclusive dep. 4 3 p.m.
D Via Retford
d Dep. 4 26 p.m. on Fridays
E Except Saturdays
F Except Saturday nights. Applies also on Sunday nights
J Arr. 3 minutes *earlier*
K Change at Radcliffe-on-Trent
L Dep. 3 10 p.m on Fridays and Saturdays
N Dep. 12 58 p.m. on Wednesdays and 2 35 p.m. on Saturdays
n Dep. 12 18 p.m. on 13th September
P On Fridays, dep. Edinburgh 10 10 a.m., Newcastle 12 59, and York 2 50 p.m. On Saturdays dep. Edinburgh 10 27 a.m. Newcastle 1 15 and York 3 10 p.m.
p p.m.
R Arr. 4 minutes *earlier*
T Change at Bottesford
t Dep. Hull 10 50 a.m. and Doncaster 1 2 p.m. on 5th July and 13th September
TC Through Carriages
U Via Market Rasen and Lincoln.
V Except Saturday nights. On Fridays until 22nd August inclusive dep. Hull 11 35, Bradford 11 33 p.m., and Leeds 12 5 ngt. On Sundays dep. Hull 9 15, Bradford 9 49, and Leeds (Central) 10 3 p.m. Passengers can also dep. Leeds (City) 11 15 p.m. via York
X Runs 5 minutes *earlier* on Saturdays.
Y Except Saturday nights. Dep. 11 55 p.m. on Sundays
Z Dep. 2 35 p.m. on Fridays also on Saturdays 12th July to 6th September inclusive
‡ Except Fridays and Saturdays. Via Louth

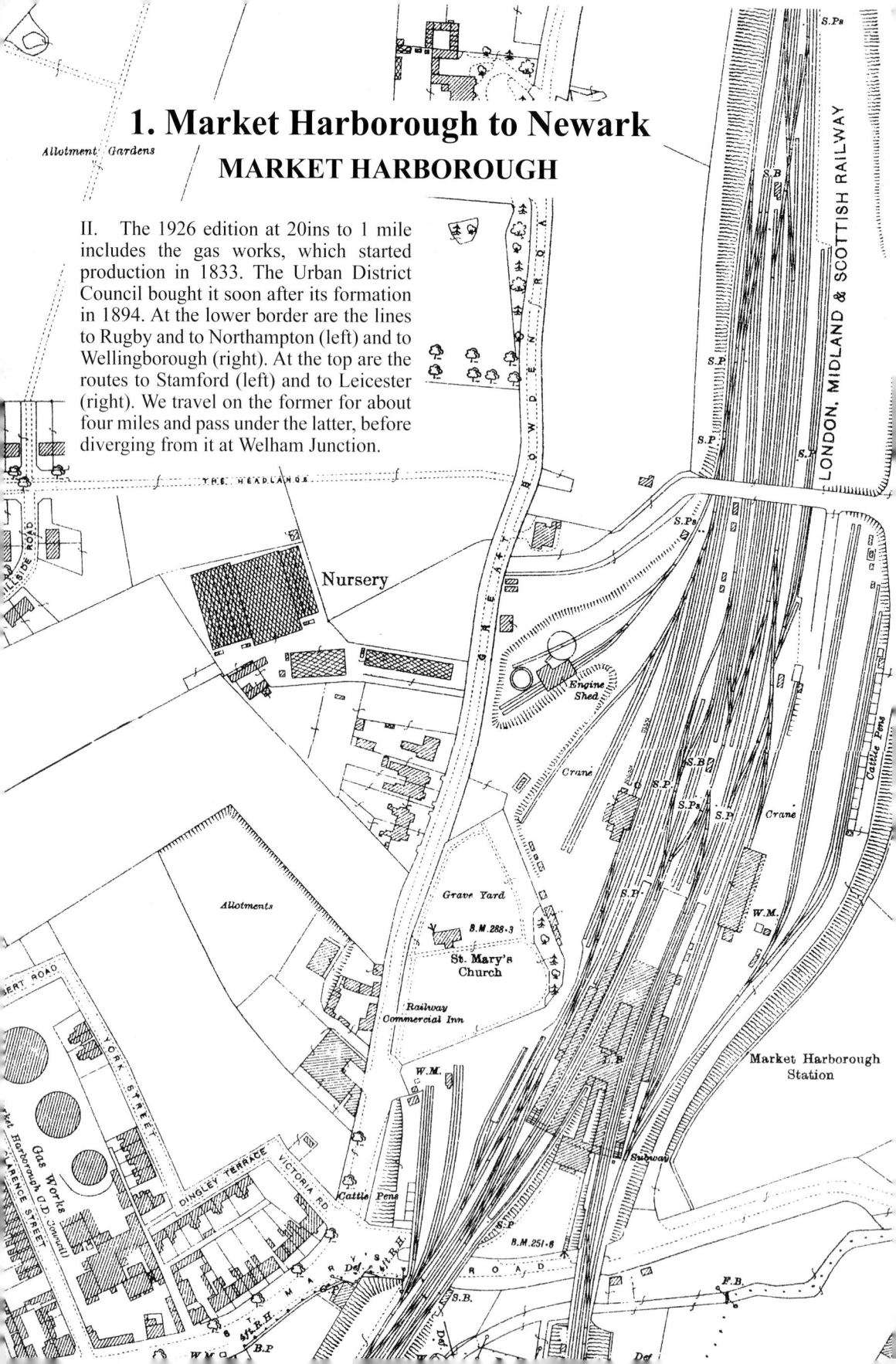

1. Market Harborough to Newark
MARKET HARBOROUGH

II. The 1926 edition at 20ins to 1 mile includes the gas works, which started production in 1833. The Urban District Council bought it soon after its formation in 1894. At the lower border are the lines to Rugby and to Northampton (left) and to Wellingborough (right). At the top are the routes to Stamford (left) and to Leicester (right). We travel on the former for about four miles and pass under the latter, before diverging from it at Welham Junction.

Allotment Gardens

THE HEADLANDS

Nursery

Allotments

Engine Shed

Crane

S.B.

S.P.

S.P.s

S.P.

Crane

W.M.

Grave Yard

B.M.288·3

St. Mary's Church

Railway Commercial Inn

W.M.

Market Harborough Station

Subway

Gas Works

DINGLEY TERRACE

VICTORIA RD.

YORK STREET

Cattle Pens

B.M.251·6

S.B.

F.B.

LONDON, MIDLAND & SCOTTISH RAILWAY

Cattle Pens

1.   This is the south elevation of the 1886 building, which was created jointly by the LNWR and the MR. Its predecessor had been of LNWR origin. A notable resident nearby had been a wood turner called Thomas Cook. He became the first person to organise a railway excursion and went on to create an international travel business. (LOSA)

2.   We are at the south end of the station, with part of the main building on the right. The site became an important one for railway observers, as six routes converged here. The town had 4400 residents in 1861, but no sewers until 1883. (Stations UK)

3.	A view from the north end has the goods shed beyond the brick wall (right) in this 1953 photo and a London-bound express arriving. The 1931 North Box is featured. It had 55 levers. (Stations UK)

4.	Class 9F 2-10-0 no. 92102 is arriving from the south on the Kettering line on 28th February 1959. It is viewed from a Northampton bound train waiting to depart from the bay platform, evident on the right of picture 2. (J.Langford)

5.   A southward view from 1964 has the 1857 Kettering lines on the left and on the right is the route which soon divides to form the 1850 lines to Rugby and the 1859 link with Northampton. (Stations UK)

Other more recent views can be found in our *Wellingborough to Leicester* **album.**

6.   It was slightly misty on 5th March 1966 and there is a smoky exhaust coming from no. D5389 as it runs north, near North Box. This closed on 20th October 1968. The main building and the subway were still in good condition in 2015. (Milepost 92½)

Market Harborough
Engine Shed

7.   This undated panorama from the road bridge allows a view through the engine shed. The map shows the turntable north of the shed, but a larger one was provided south of it, in about 1930. It was 60ft long. The ash pit was added in about 1920 and the water softener (left) came in 1947. (Colour-Rail.com)

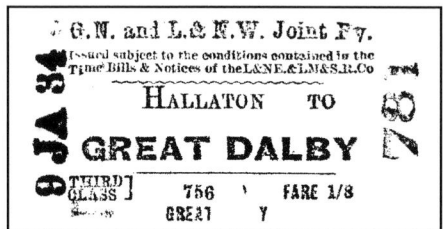

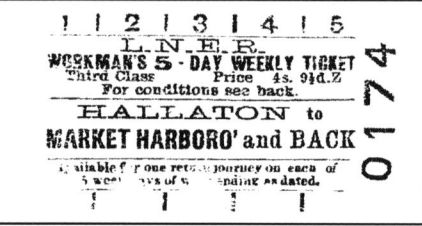

8.   This view dated 12th March 1961 shows that the shed roof was provided by its water tank. The coaling area was given a roof, probably during World War II, when many were added as a blackout precaution. The turntable road is on the left. (Colour-Rail.com)

9.   The shed code was 2F in 1955-58 and 15F in 1958-60, but otherwise it was a sub-shed. By that period, it housed only four engines. Six was often the number in the 1920s. The shed is seen in 1965, at the time of its closure. (R.S.Carpenter)

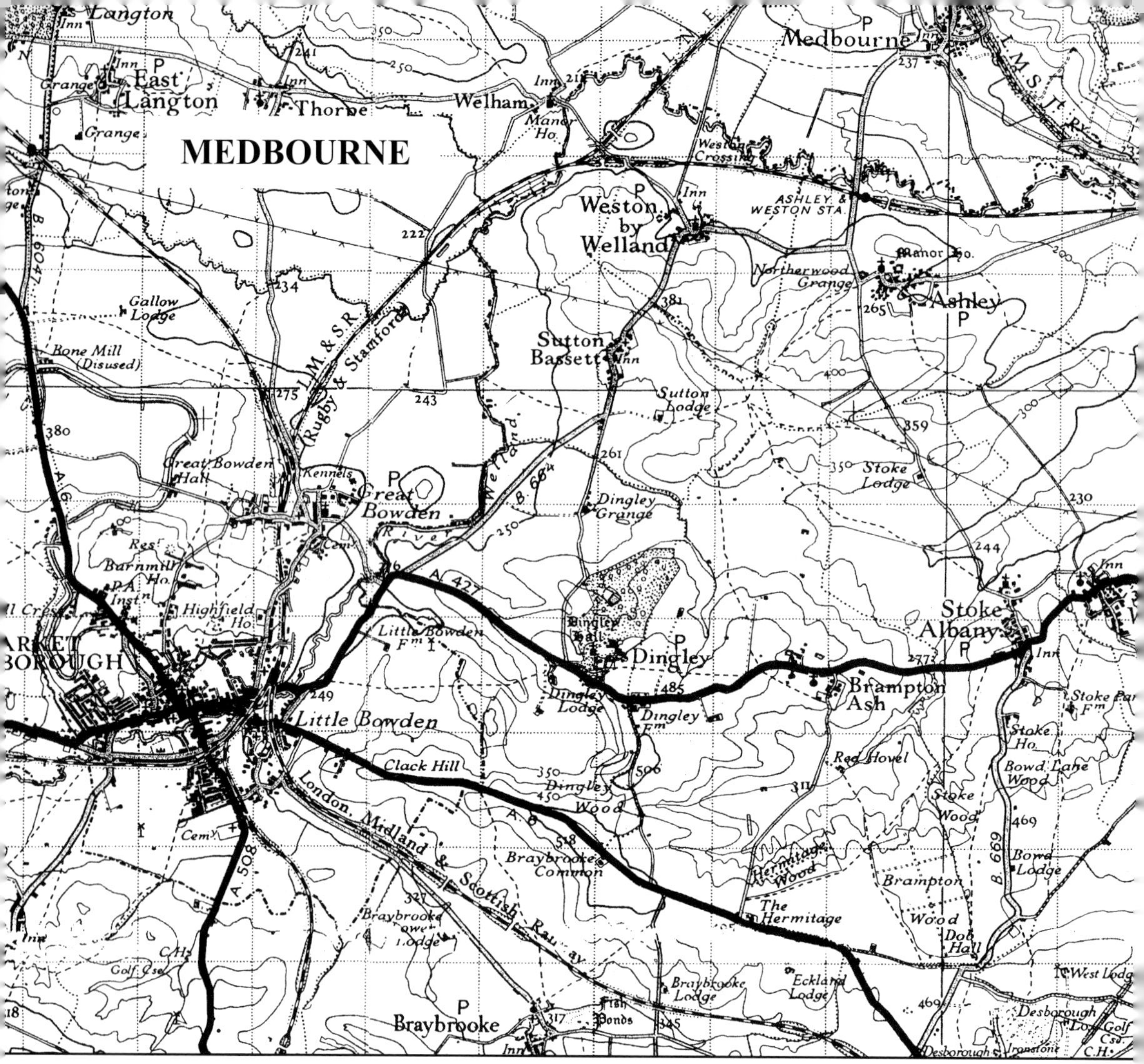

MEDBOURNE

III. The station was on the eastern part of the triangle, the left of which is on our route north. The station opened on 2nd July 1883 and closed on 1st April 1916, along with its side of the triangle. However, it appears on this 1946 survey, which is at 1ins to 1 mile. It seems that one track was reopened for goods after 1918. It was not used for goods traffic during 1939-45, but was used to store the Royal Train. The line on the right runs to Stamford and is close to Drayton Junction. Hallaton Junction is beyond the top border and Welham Junction is near the village of that name. There are sidings nearby.

10. Sadly, the main building was destroyed by fire soon after its closure. There were no foot crossings, passengers using the road bridge. The population was 427 in 1901 and 374 in 1961. (J.Langford coll.)

11.   The station to the south of the village was called Ashley & Weston, having been renamed from Medbourne Bridge, some five years before Medbourne opened. This is the final station house and is seen in June 1959. (J.Langford)

IV. The 1902 edition is at 12ins to 1 mile.

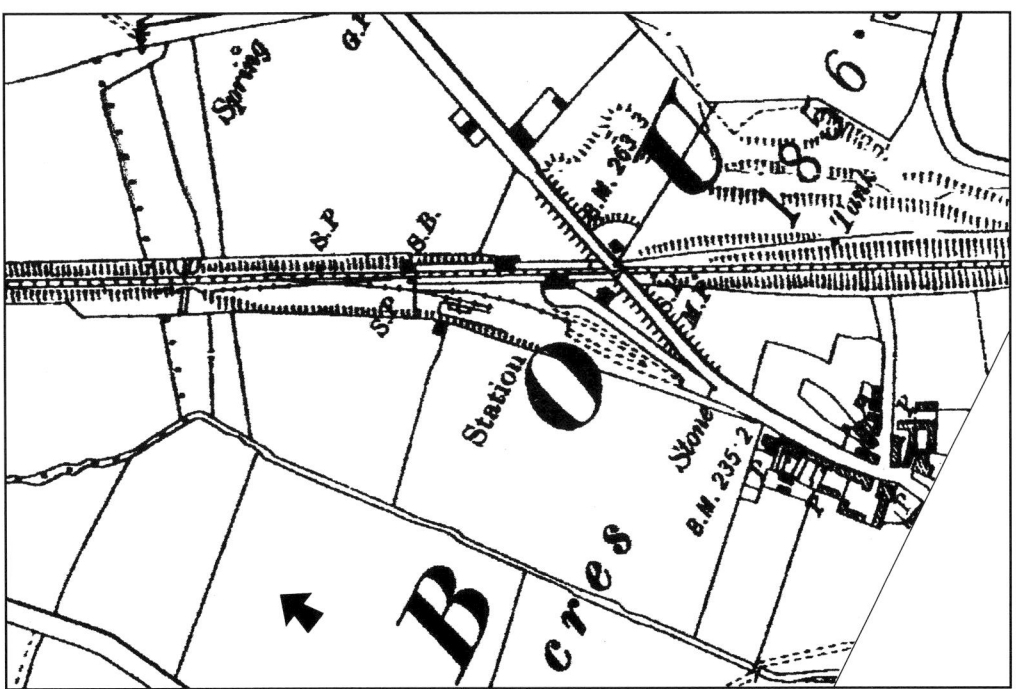

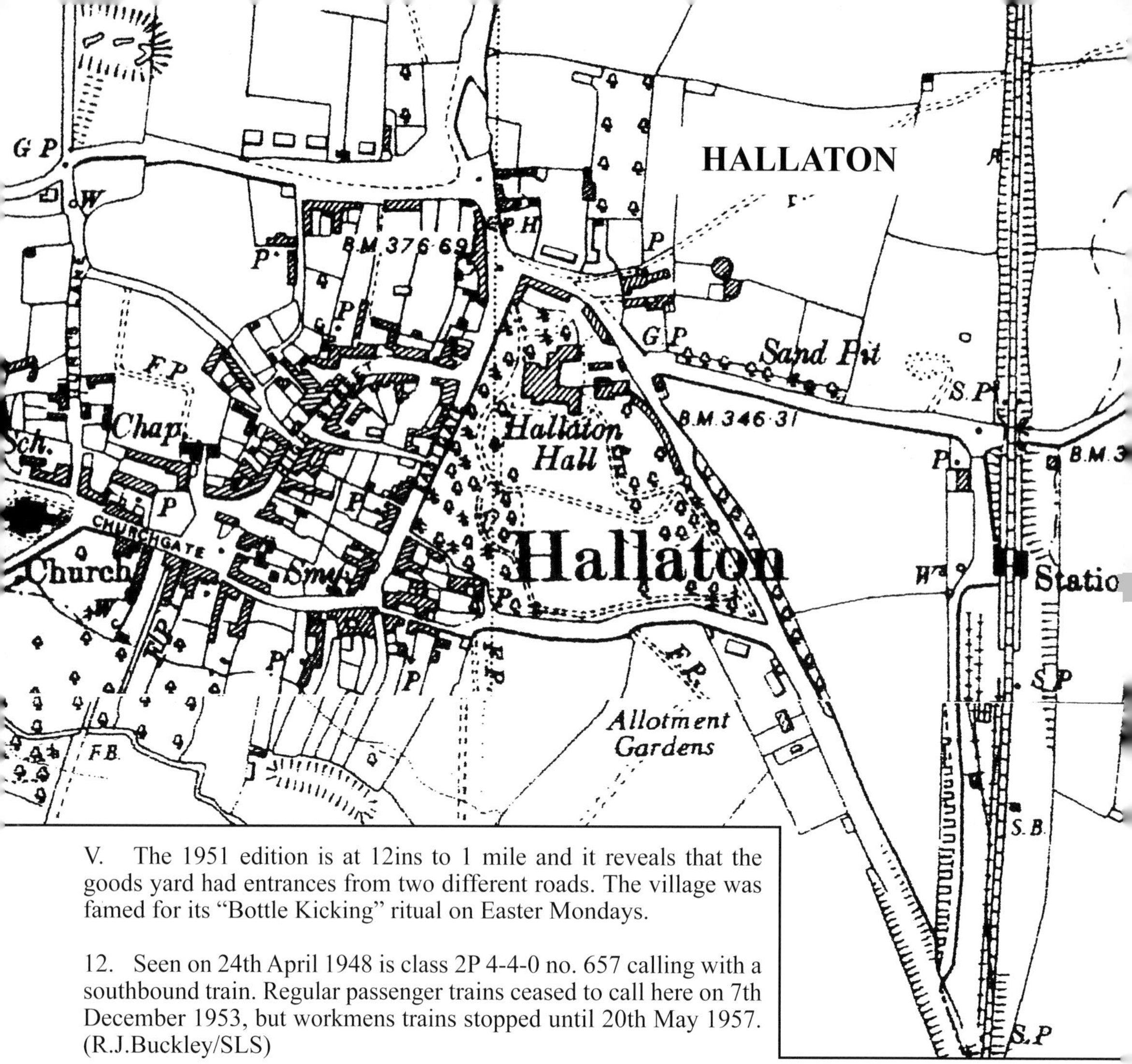

V. The 1951 edition is at 12ins to 1 mile and it reveals that the goods yard had entrances from two different roads. The village was famed for its "Bottle Kicking" ritual on Easter Mondays.

12. Seen on 24th April 1948 is class 2P 4-4-0 no. 657 calling with a southbound train. Regular passenger trains ceased to call here on 7th December 1953, but workmens trains stopped until 20th May 1957. (R.J.Buckley/SLS)

13.   A photo from 6th August 1953 includes the signal box, which was in use from 1912 until 1958. It had 18 levers and is opposite the goods yard, which was in use until 4th November 1957. It had received large quantities of lineside hay for fodder for many years. (R.M.Casserley)

14.   The Casserley's 1934 Hillman 10 often enhanced photographs, this one being from 11th May 1962, when it was at risk from an insecure soffit board. A hoard of more than 5000 gold and silver coins dating to the late iron age was found near the village in 2000. (R.M.Casserley)

15. This survey was from the same day and is the view northwards. It includes the stationmasters dwelling, on the left. The population had dropped from 602 in 1901 to 424 in 1961. (R.M.Casserley)

16. We look in the other direction on 7th December 1959. The LMS running-in boards were known as "Hawkseyes". The colour contrasts differ in picture 13. (J.Langford)

EAST NORTON

VI. The 1902 survey at 6ins to 1 mile has at the top the viaduct illustrated in picture 21. The straight road down to the goods yard is to the left of the station. There were 149 residents in 1901 and just 95 in 1961.

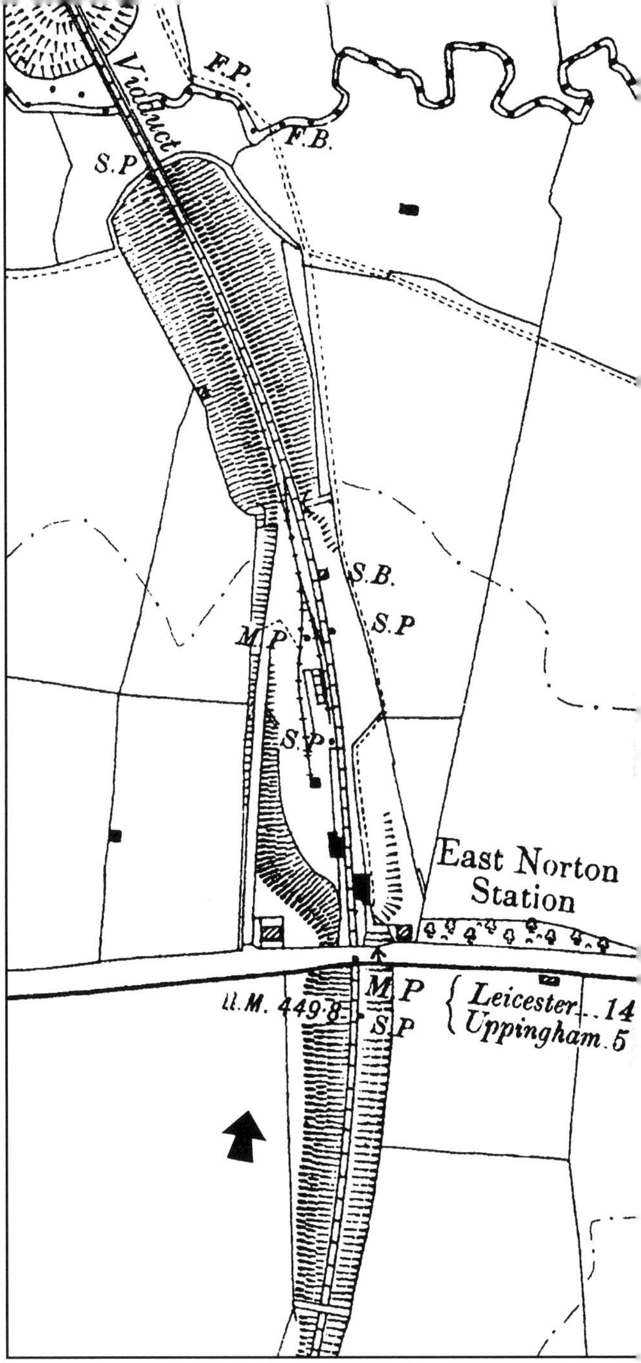

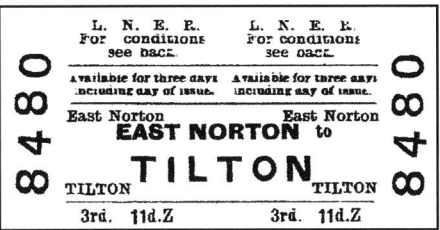

17. A view south shows formwork under one of the arches of the road bridge. It has either just been constructed or has developed a fault and needs support. The churns are a reminder of the need to send milk to Melton Mowbray to make cheese. (LOSA)

18. The house for the stationmaster offered good views over the station, in the interest of security. Pedestrian access is evident, but heavy luggage or milk churns had to be taken to the other platform over the barrow crossing. (LOSA)

19. It is 24th April 1948 and class 2P 4-4-0 no. 657 is working the 2.43pm Market Harborough to Nottingham service. Road vehicle access to the down platform is on the right. The three railway cottages were demolished in 2007. (SLS coll.)

20. This panorama is from 10th October 1959 and includes most of the goods yard, left. This was in use until 4th November 1963. Passenger service was withdrawn on 7th December 1953, but the workmens trains between Market Harborough and here continued until 20th May 1957. It had been secured by the Billesden Rural District Council. The 1912 20-lever signal box was closed on 4th November 1963. (Milepost 92½)

21. The viaduct is at the top of the map, but one could see little of it in September 1973. It had 13 spans, eight of which were brick arches. The nearby cuttings were filled with rubbish and the 190m long structure was blown up in March 2001. (M.J.Stretton)

TILTON

VII. The 1884 edition is at 6ins to 1 mile. Later was a crane, which was rated at 5 tons capacity. There were 128 residents in 1901 and 375 in 1961. The staff had comprised the stationmaster, three porters and two signalmen.

22. The digging of the cutting south of the station (foreground) revealed substantial beds of ironstone, which soon had to be transported away by rail, from a new pit (top centre). Daily, 25 wagon loads was common practice and the destination was Holwell Iron Works, north of Melton Mowbray. Traffic began in 1880 with a zig-zag standard gauge track from the quarry. Narrow gauge had come by 1912 and was used until 1950, when digging started east of the main line. A Bailey Bridge was built over it, so that quarry vehicles could take the ore to the existing sidings. Ore traffic ceased in 1961; passenger carriage ended on 7th December 1953 and general goods ceased on 4th November 1963. The 1883 signal box had 28 levers and closed then. (J.S.Gilks/M.J.Stretton)

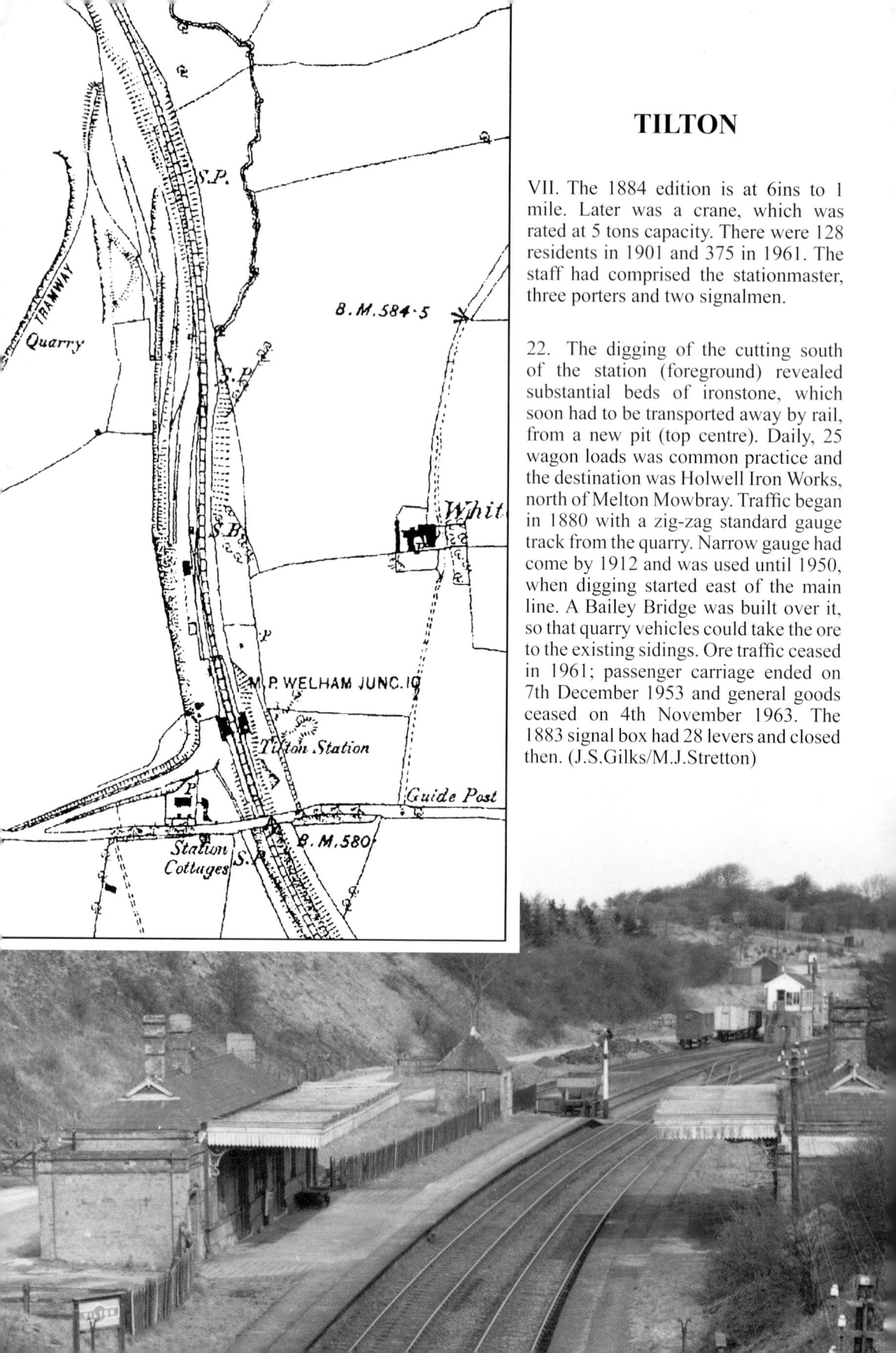

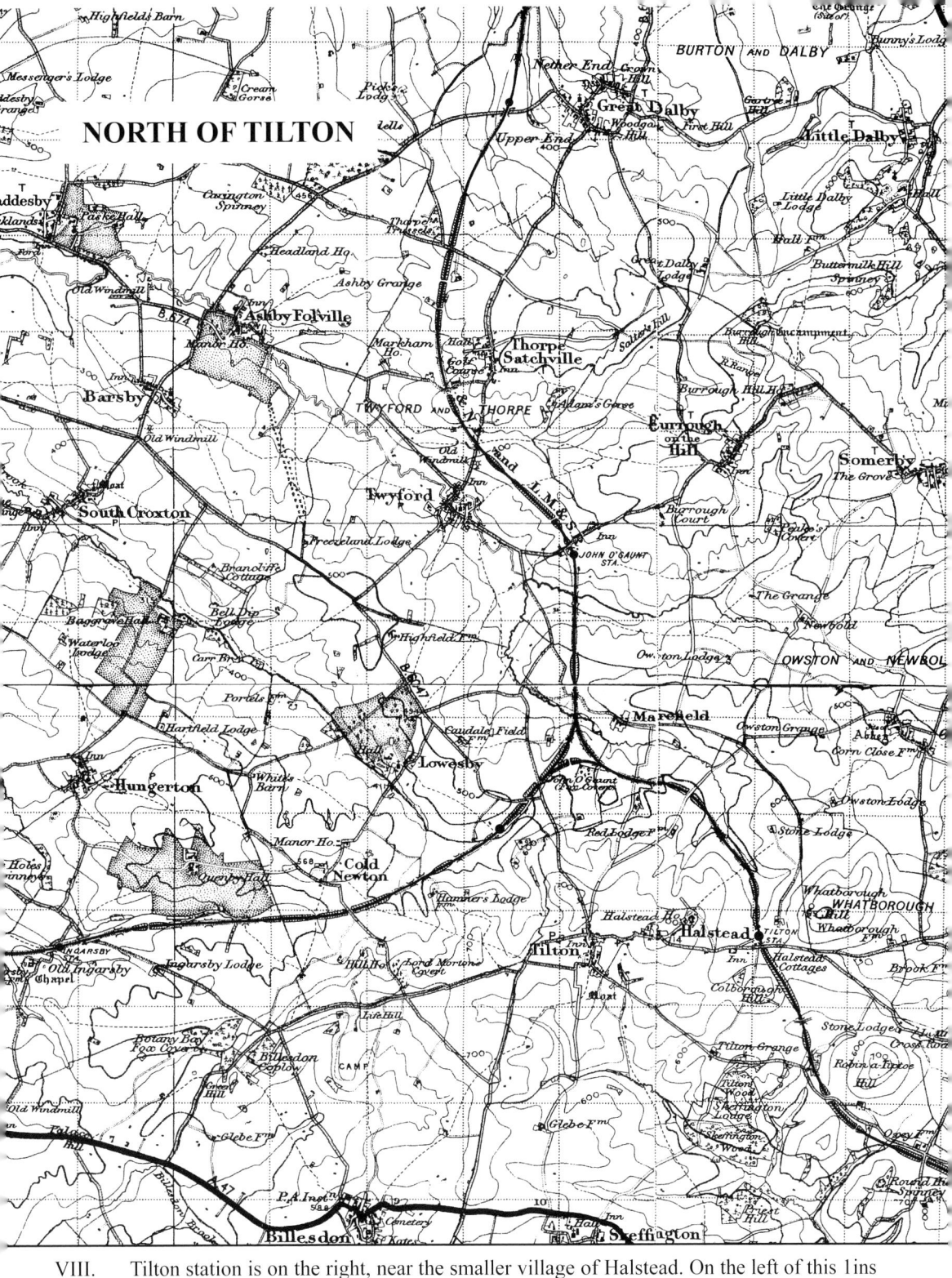

VIII.   Tilton station is on the right, near the smaller village of Halstead. On the left of this 1ins to 1 mile map from 1947 is the branch to Leicester Belgrave Road, opened in 1883. Its first station is southeast of Lowesby and it is illustrated in pictures 94-97, with the branch following.

23. This 1968 southward view has the route to Market Harborough on the left and the one to Leicester Belgrave Road on the right. The box had 20 levers and was called Marefield North Junction until South Junction box closed in 1930. Closure came with the line to Leicester on 26th February 1964. The southern curve closed on 1st April 1916 and never reopened.
(T.G.Hepburn/Rail Archive Stephenson)

Marefield Junction Boxes

	Levers	Opened	Closed
South	15	1882	1930
North	20	1911	1964
West	20	1882	1931

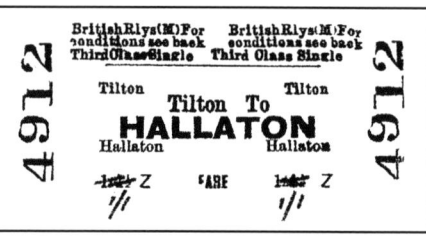

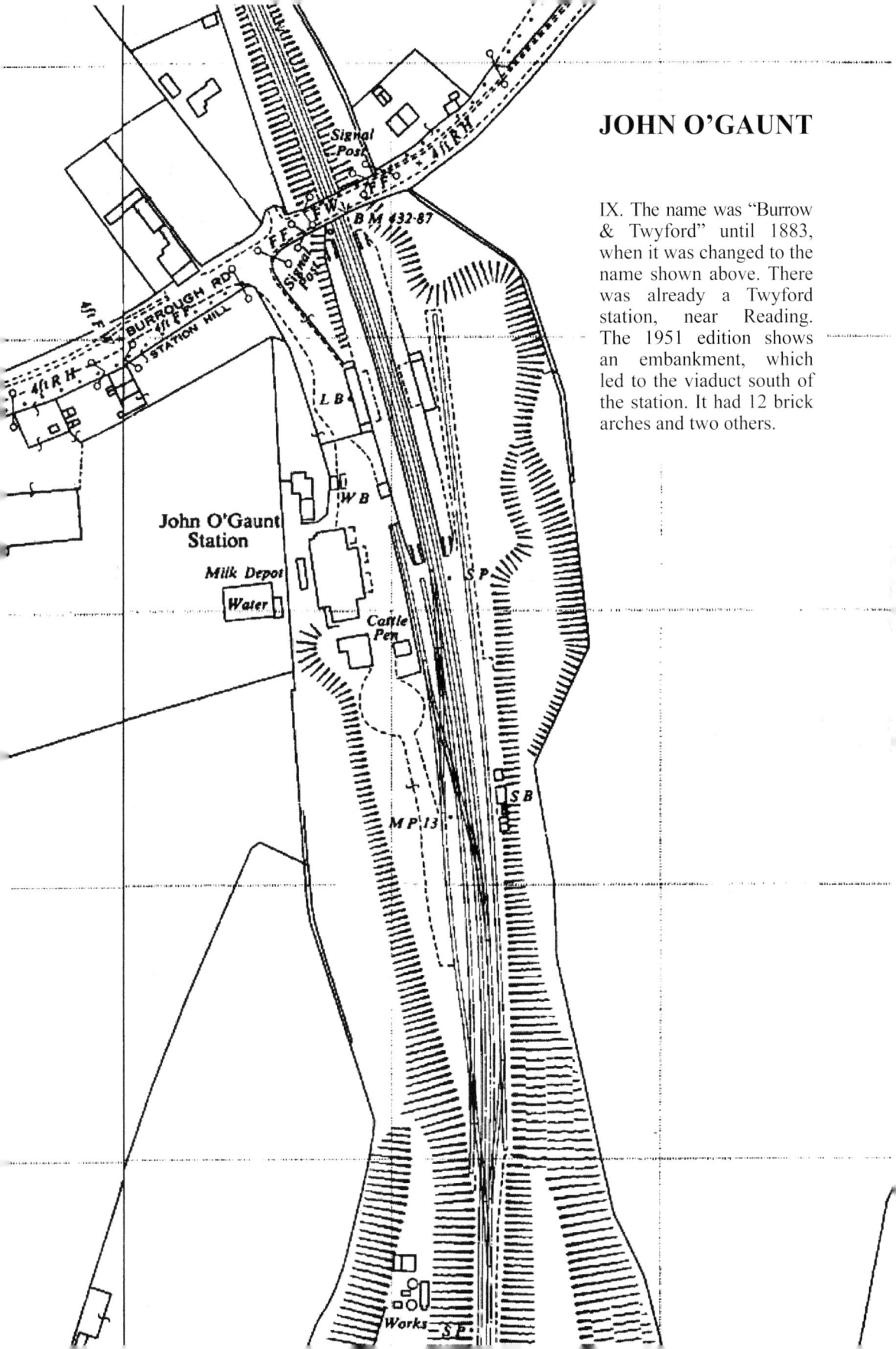

JOHN O'GAUNT

IX. The name was "Burrow & Twyford" until 1883, when it was changed to the name shown above. There was already a Twyford station, near Reading. The 1951 edition shows an embankment, which led to the viaduct south of the station. It had 12 brick arches and two others.

Signal Post

B M 432·87

Signal Post

BURROUGH RD

4 FT F

STATION HILL

4 FT R H

L B

W B

John O'Gaunt Station

Milk Depot

Water

Cattle Pen

S P

S B

M P 13

Works S B

24. The 1.55pm to Leicester was photographed on 10th January 1942. No. 4166 was a class J3 0-6-0, a type introduced in 1896, by the GNR. Closure to passengers came on 29th April 1957, when the Leicester workmens service ceased. (H.C.Casserley)

25. It is 4th April 1948 and class 2P 4-4-0 no. 419 is heading the 10.38am Nottingham to Northampton service. The roofless part (right) was for the benefit of gentlemen. (W.A.Camwell/SLS)

26. Coal wagons almost fill the background as a northbound train calls. Goods traffic ceased here on 4th November 1963. Agricultural crops were varied and heavy, but inevitably seasonal. (LOSA)

27. A view south in August 1959 includes the milk depot (right). Initially, milk was despatched in 16 gallon cans, but tankers arrived in the 1930s and 8000 gallons were often loaded per day. On Sundays, in the later years, a milk special started here and ran to Rugby. (M.J.Stretton coll.)

28. An East Coast holiday train runs through on 8th July 1961, while the signalman's transport waits under the canopy. The station approach can be seen between the buildings. (R.Joanes)

29. This is a southward panorama from 19th March 1962 and the wagons in the distance are probably in store awaiting their demise. The signal box lasted until 4th December 1963, its frame having 30 levers. (M.J.Stretton coll.)

GREAT DALBY

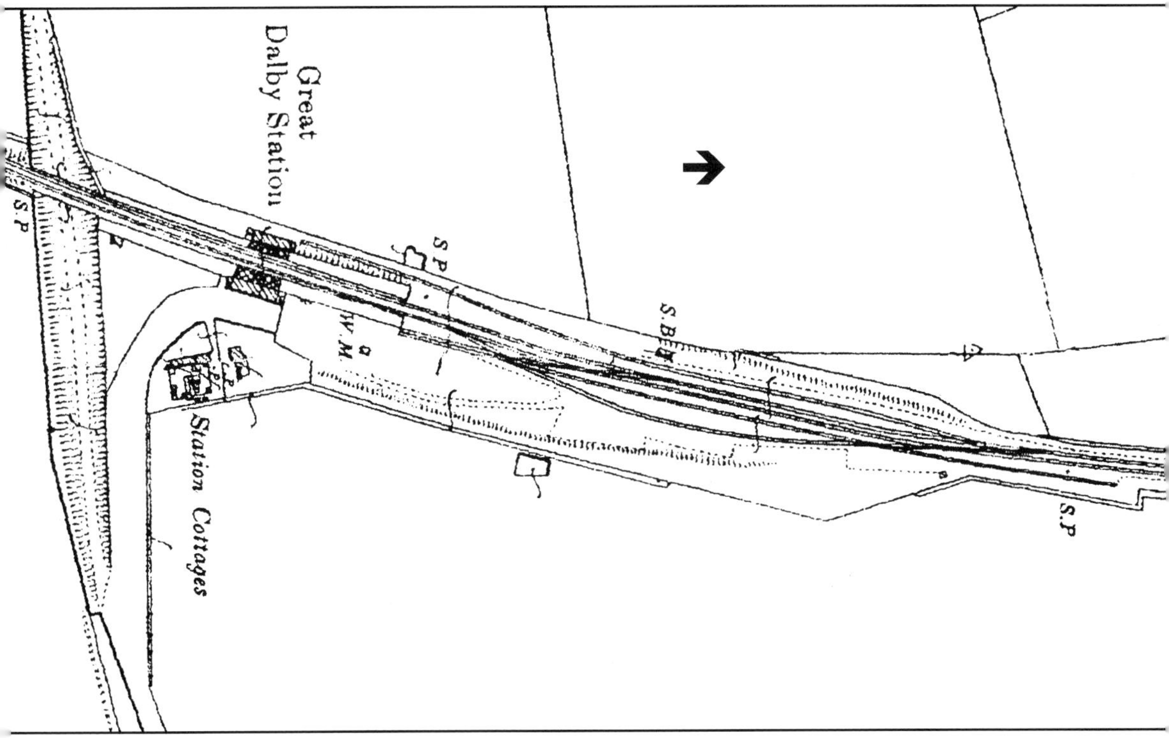

X.   The village housed 356 in 1901 and 321 in 1961. The 1904 edition is at about 15ins to 1 mile.

30.   This 1930s northward photo does not come with any data. Unusual details include the step for staff crossing and the framing for lamp support. (Stations UK)

31.   The spacious signal box was pictured in 1956, with windows smashed. It had opened in 1897 and its 30-lever frame was taken out of use on 7th December 1953, although local goods traffic continued until 4th November 1963. (Colour-Rail.com)

32.   Local passenger trains ceased on 7th December 1953, but East Coast holiday trains continued to grace the scene. This is the 1.20pm (S.O.) Skegness to Leicester Belgrave Road on 25th June 1960, hauled by class B1 4-6-0 no. 61163. (M.J.Stretton coll.)

33.   During the later part of World War II, the US Army stored ammunition in the area and after D-Day, the yard was hectic with its loading. Milk churns had earlier caused two busy periods each day on the platforms. This is their state in March 1962. (M.J.Stretton coll.)

34.   Nature was in charge by the time no. 43156 was recorded on 7th July 1962. This was a class 4MT 2-6-0, one of 162 built from 1947 onwards. Freight trains regularly used this line from the north to avoid Leicester. (Colour-Rail.com)

MELTON MOWBRAY

XI. Our journey is from the lower border to the top one, over this 1947 extract at 1ins to 1 mile. The Leicester & Peterborough line, built by the MR, is west-east and branching north from it at Sysonby is the present test track. This and Melton's southern station are featured in our *Kettering to Nottingham* album. There was a north-east mineral connection in 1883-87.

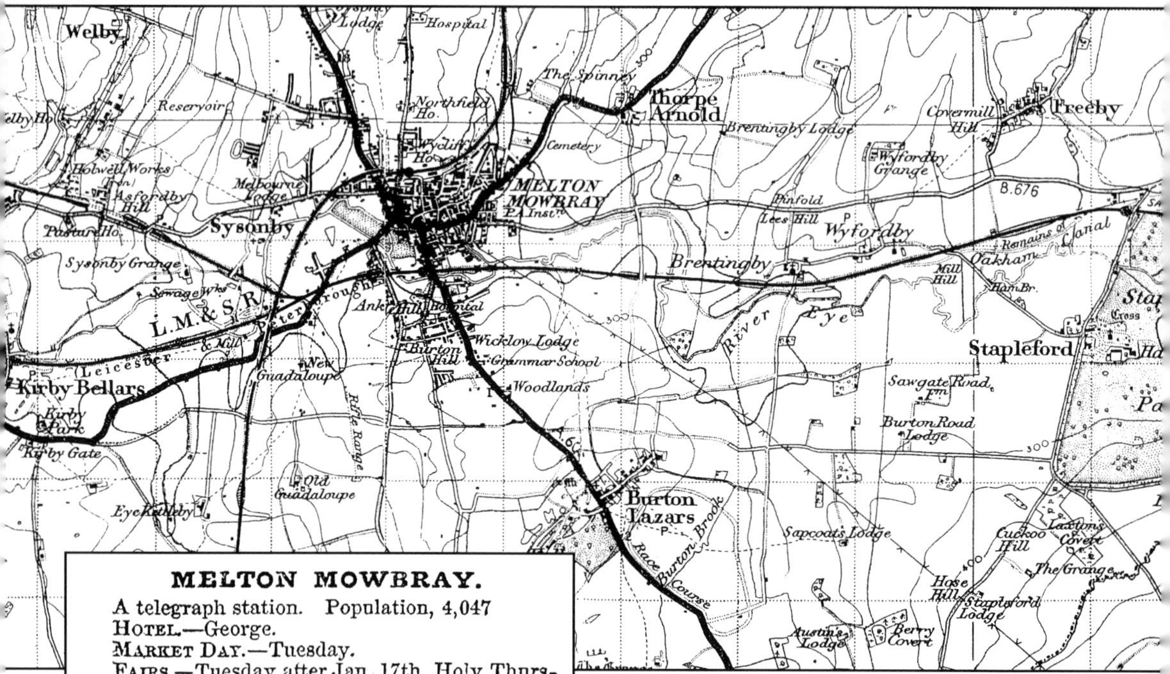

MELTON MOWBRAY.

A telegraph station.   Population, 4,047
HOTEL.—George.
MARKET DAY.—Tuesday.
FAIRS.—Tuesday after Jan. 17th, Holy Thursday, Whit Tuesday, and August 21st.
MELTON MOWBRAY is the centre of a famous hunting country. Horses are bred here: its pork pies and Stilton cheese are also valuable productions. All about this quarter is excellent pasture for superior breeds of stock, well known as Leicestershire, especially the old or short-horned cattle and the new Leicestershire sheep, a large long-woolled breed. The cheeses are flat, weighing 30 to 50lbs. each. *Mowbray Lodge*, seat of General Wyndham.

35. This postcard shows the station approach from Scalford Road, which is on the left of the next map. "Northern Station" was the description used, although "North" was only officially applied to its goods yard from 1st July 1950. It appeared on East Coast timetables and some tickets from 18th June 1962, but only for a few weeks. (P.Laming coll.)

36. The GN and LNW Joint Railway established its line superintendents office here. Initially, there were 1st, 2nd and 3rd class waiting rooms, plus a dining room. Its kitchen and staff rooms were below the platforms. The roof glazing was dangerous and eventually removed. (Stations UK)

XII. The 1930 edition at 20ins to 1 mile shows the close proximity of the cattle market (lower left)to the station, some pens being evident at the left border. Cattle pens are also near the northern siding.

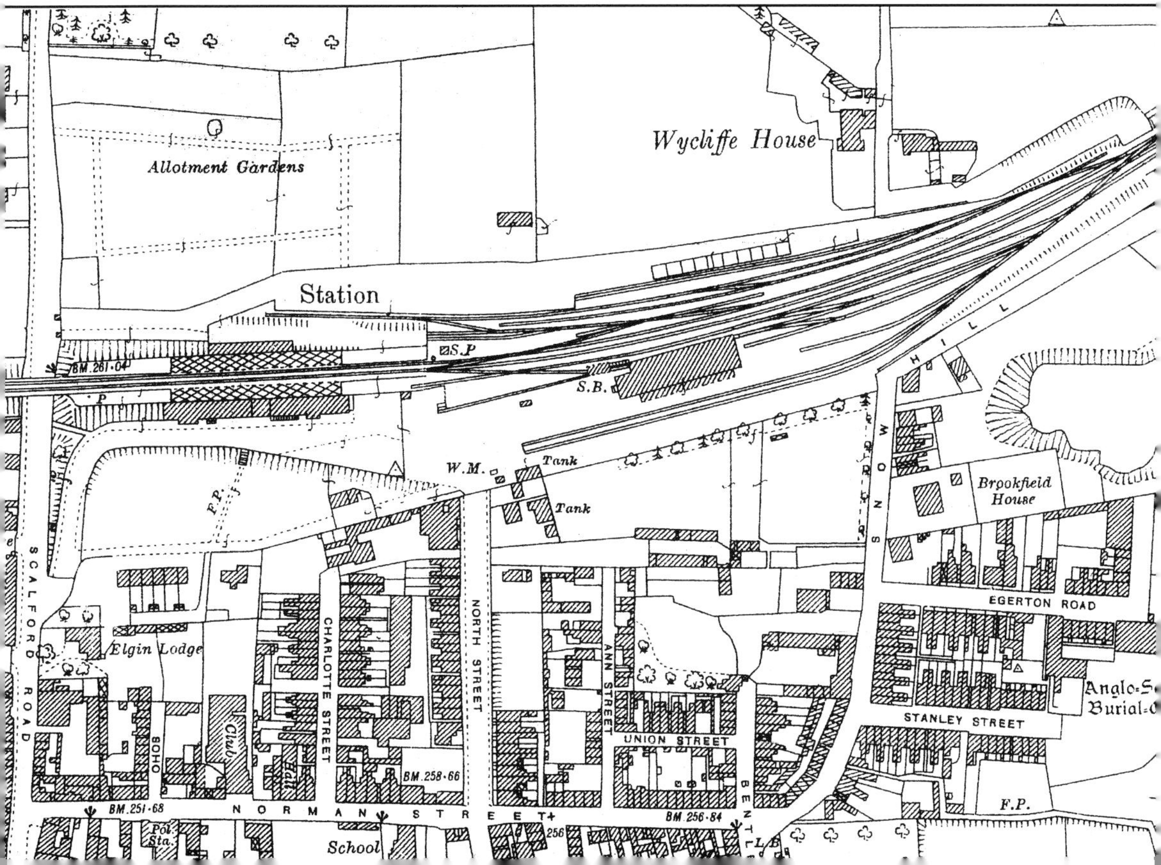

37.   Seen on 24th April 1948 is class 3 2-6-2T no. 52. It would soon receive BR no. 40052. In peace time years, the station was often very busy with hunt traffic. The station was also noted for its traffic in locally produced cheese of great fame. (R.J.Buckley/Initial Photographics)

38.   Departing on the same day is ex-LMS class 2P 4-4-0 no. 657 working the 7.28am to Northampton. In the distance is the 1914 signal box, described in caption 44.
(R.J.Buckley/Initial Photographics)

39.   An architectural study from 22nd August 1953 features the former entrance to the 2nd class refreshment room and decorated columns to the white glazed brick entrance to the subway. Unclear above it is the coat of arms of one of the joint companies. (H.C.Casserley)

40.   Sadly undated, this view includes one of the holidaymaker's expresses, with class B1 4-6-0 no. 61177 at its head, eastbound. The short dock is on the left. There was a 5-ton crane in the goods yard. (N.Stead/M.J.Stretton)

41.   A typical mixed freight of the early 1950s is seen behind class 8F 2-8-0 no. 48398. An amazing 852 were built between 1935 and 1946. The 1938 handbook listed an LMS engineers yard here and also Wagon Repairs Ltd. (A.Ford/M.J.Stretton)

42.   Devoid of posters, seats and lights, the station is about to receive passengers from East Coast resorts on 8th July 1961. Hauling the train to Leicester Belgrave Road is Eastern Region class B1 4-6-0 no. 61088. (R.Joanes)

43. Bedford and Ford vans are in attendance. We can enjoy the architectural details, which include more company crests. Horse delivery vans were used until 1950. Earlier, the hunts had used 20 to 30 horse boxes to bring their performers. No trace of this building remains. (Colour-Rail.com)

44. There were "South" and "North" boxes until replaced by this 48-lever box in 1914. The first used LNWR systems and the other ran on GNR practices. Closure came on 29th May 1964. Class B1 4-6-0 no. 61285 accelerates a Leicester to Skegness service on 11th August 1962. (T.G.Hepburn/Rail Archive Stephenson)

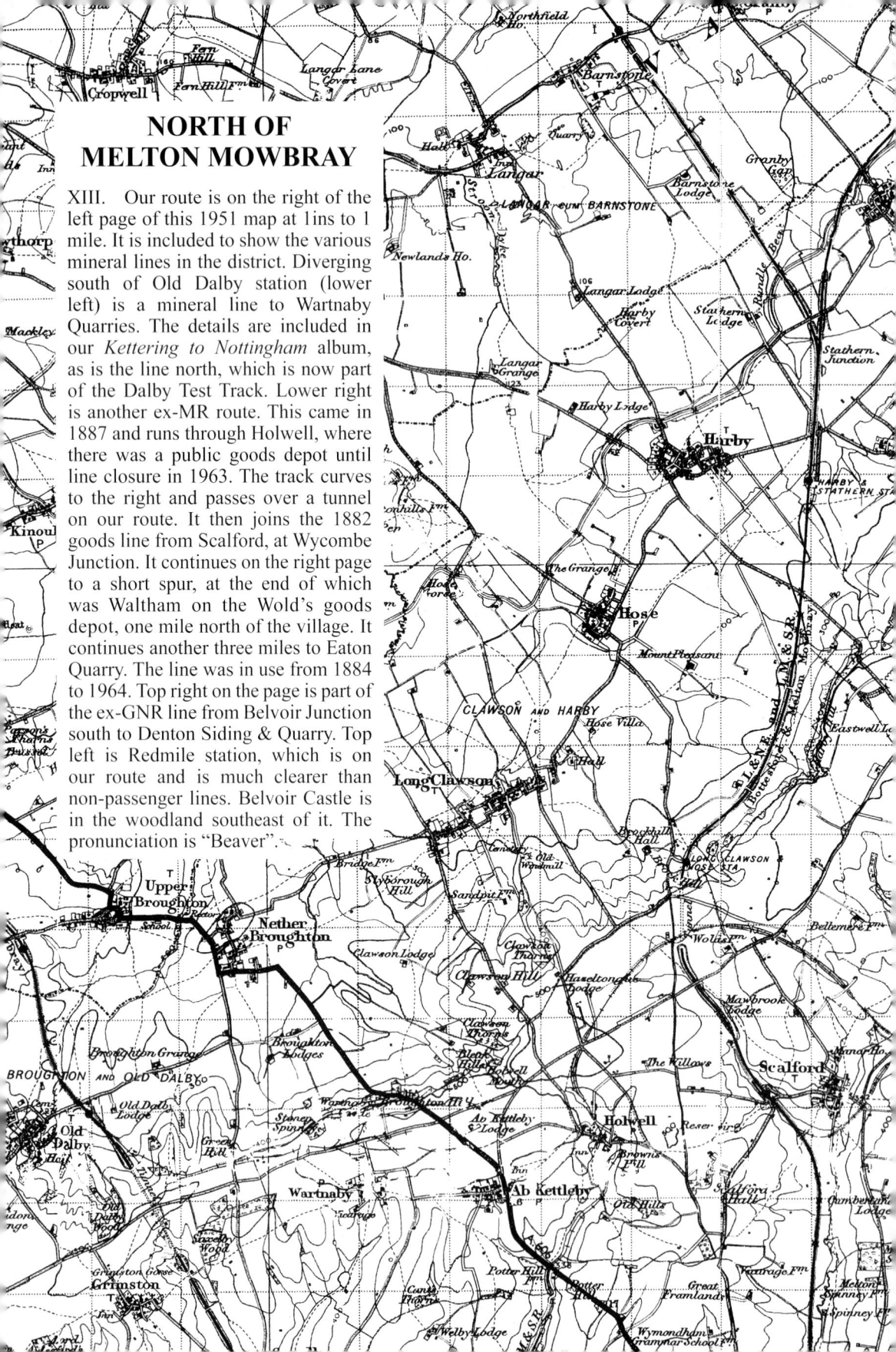

NORTH OF MELTON MOWBRAY

XIII. Our route is on the right of the left page of this 1951 map at 1ins to 1 mile. It is included to show the various mineral lines in the district. Diverging south of Old Dalby station (lower left) is a mineral line to Wartnaby Quarries. The details are included in our *Kettering to Nottingham* album, as is the line north, which is now part of the Dalby Test Track. Lower right is another ex-MR route. This came in 1887 and runs through Holwell, where there was a public goods depot until line closure in 1963. The track curves to the right and passes over a tunnel on our route. It then joins the 1882 goods line from Scalford, at Wycombe Junction. It continues on the right page to a short spur, at the end of which was Waltham on the Wold's goods depot, one mile north of the village. It continues another three miles to Eaton Quarry. The line was in use from 1884 to 1964. Top right on the page is part of the ex-GNR line from Belvoir Junction south to Denton Siding & Quarry. Top left is Redmile station, which is on our route and is much clearer than non-passenger lines. Belvoir Castle is in the woodland southeast of it. The pronunciation is "Beaver".

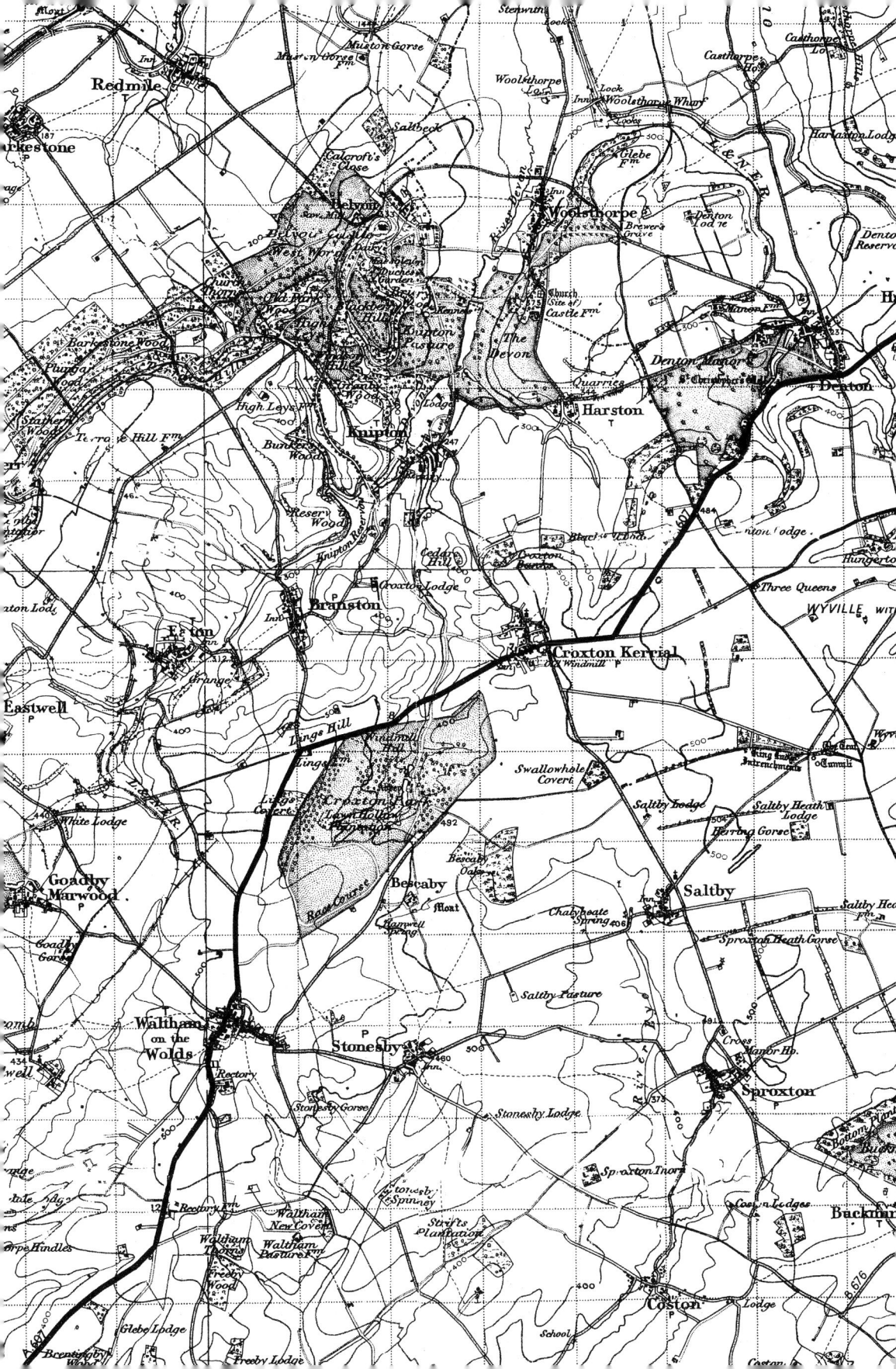

Wycombe Junction

45. Wycombe Junction was where the MR line ended and joined the 1882 GNR goods route. The box is seen from a special bound for Waltham on the Wold on 16th May 1953. The 15-lever box of 1887 closed on 27th July 1963. (H.C.Casserley)

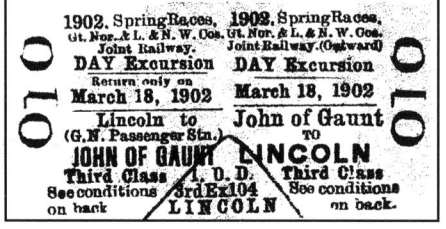

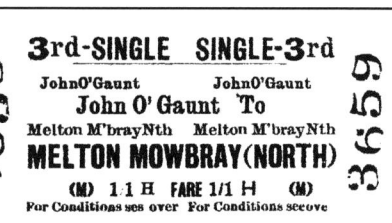

46.   The signals are ex-GNR Somersault type. The 1890 box is seen from the same train. It had 16 levers and was in use until 4th May 1964. The straight line had been completed in 1882 and the Holwell Iron Co. loaded ore at the end of it. (R.S.Carpenter coll.)

47. A panorama from 1953 reveals the unusually extensive space available and that the usual fencing was not required. The Holwell mineral line had once continued under the bridge. Tipping facilities can be seen on the right. (LOSA)

48. An SLS railtour arrived on 16th May 1953 and is seen behind class 2 2-6-0 no. 46443. The train started at Derby Midland and ran via Ambergate, Mansfield, Newark and Nottingham. (R.S.Carpenter coll.)

49.   The high level siding can be found on the left. It had originally been arranged for end tipping of ore from Waltham Quarry's 3ft 1ins gauge horse-drawn wagons. (R.O.Tuck/M.J.Stretton)

50.   Seen on 29th May 1960 is class O1 2-8-0 no. 63594, with a cattle truck forming part of a pick-up goods. The platform had earlier been used occasionally by specials for hunting parties. (R.O.Tuck/M.J.Stretton)

Eastwell and Eaton Quarries

51.   The Waltham on the Wold branch was built to serve various ironstone quarries, all of which had their own internal tramways, usually narrow gauge. The best known and longest lived was the 3ft gauge system serving Eastwell Quarries and the metre gauge serving Eaton (Waltham) quarries. From the latter was *Dreadnought*, a large 0-4-2ST from Manning Wardle built in 1914; originally an 0-4-0ST, it was rebuilt with an extra trailing truck in 1935. (A.Neale coll.)

52.   This rather ugly cabless 0-4-0ST was one of a handful of industrial steam locomotives built by Markham & Co. of Chesterfield, better known for their steam winding engines. It was photographed when lying derelict and awaiting scrapping on 25th August 1960. Built in 1889, it was named *The Baronet*. (M.C.Fayers/A.Neale coll.)

53. Due to its unusual gauge of one metre, two Corpet 0-6-0Ts were purchased from closed railways in France in the 1930s. One of them, *Nantes*, built by Corpet Louvet in 1903 heads a loaded train in about 1954. (F.Jones/A.Neale coll.)

54. The length and heavy traffic carried by the Eastwell railway required a fleet of powerful four and six coupled locomotives. *Mountaineer* was one of two similar 0-6-0STs supplied by W.G.Bagnall Ltd of Stafford in 1923. The elevated wagon body is worthy of study. (F.Jones/A.Neale coll.)

55.   Further pictures of the Eastwell 3ft gauge tramway can be enjoyed now. A view down the two-track cable operated incline is from 29th May 1958. The early pits of 1883 were to the north of the area and the final one of 1955 to the south. (IRS/K.J.Cooper coll.)

56.   A general view of Eastwell yard shows the two locomotive sheds. Outside the left-hand one is the 1936 Hunslet 0-6-0ST *Belvoir*. Note the horizontal water tower using a redundant Cornish boiler. Eastwell can be found near the join of the two pages on the last map, along with the BR connection. (IRS/K.J.Cooper coll.)

57.   We are at the Eaton (Ropeway) Ironstone quarries. The 3ft gauge ironstone quarry line here, as the name implies, was connected to the Waltham branch by an aerial ropeway. Following replacement by road transport, scrapping took place in the summer of 1949. On 25th July 1949, the 1898 Hudswell Clark 0-4-0ST *Stanton* No.9 is partly cut up and to the rear, *Harston*, a 1900 Bagnall 0-4-0ST, awaits the same fate. The Eaton Mineral Branch was in use until 4th May 1964. (K.J.Cooper/IRS coll.)

Eastwell Iron Ore Company *3ft. Gauge*

John Green	Built by Staveley (?) in 1880; 0-4-0 saddle tank; vertical cyl; gear drive. Scrapped 1913
Belvoir	Built by Staveley (?) in 1885. 0-4-0 saddle tank; vertical cyl; gear drive. Scrapped 1920
Lord Granby	Hudswell, Clarke & Co No. 633 of 1902; 0-4-0 saddle tank. Survives.
The Scot	Hudswell Clarke & Co No. 776 of 1906; 0-4-0 saddle tank. Scrapped 1957.
Underbank	Peckett & Sons No. 873 of 1900; 0-4-0 saddle tank. Scrapped 1961.
Banshee	Manning, Wardle & Co. No. 1276 of 1894; 0-6-0 saddle tank. 1921-1928.
Woodcock	Black, Hawthorn & Co. No.1046 of 1892; 0-4-0 saddle tank. Scrapped 1948
Pioneer	W G Bagnall No. 1980 of 1913; 0-6-0 saddle tank. Scrapped 1962.
Mountaineer	W G Bagnall No. 2203 of 1923; 0-6-0 saddle tank. Scrapped 1960.
Scaldwell	Peckett & Sons No. 1316 of 1913; 0-6-0 saddle tank. 1947-1950
Belvoir	Hunslet Engine Co. No. 1823 of 1936; 0-6-0 saddle tank. Scrapped 1962.
Nancy	Avonside Engine Co. No. 1547 of 1908; 0-6-0 tank. Survives.

Waltham Iron Ore Company *Metre Gauge*

George Bond	Built by Staveley (?) in 1884; 0-4-0 saddle tank; vertical cylinders; gear driv
Rutland	Built by Staveley (?) in 1886; 0-4-0 saddle tank; vertical cylinders; gear drive
Dreadnought	Manning, Wardle & Co. No. 1757 of 1910: 0-4-0 saddle tank (later 0-4-2). Scrapped 1960
The Baronet	Markham & Co. No. 102 of 1889; 0-4-0 saddle tank. Scrapped 1960
Nantes	Corpet & Louvet No. 936 of 1903; 0-6-0 tank; Purchased 1934. Scrapped 1960.
Cambrai	L Corpet No. 493 of 1888; 0-6-0 tank; Ex-Loddington in 1956. Survives

SCALFORD

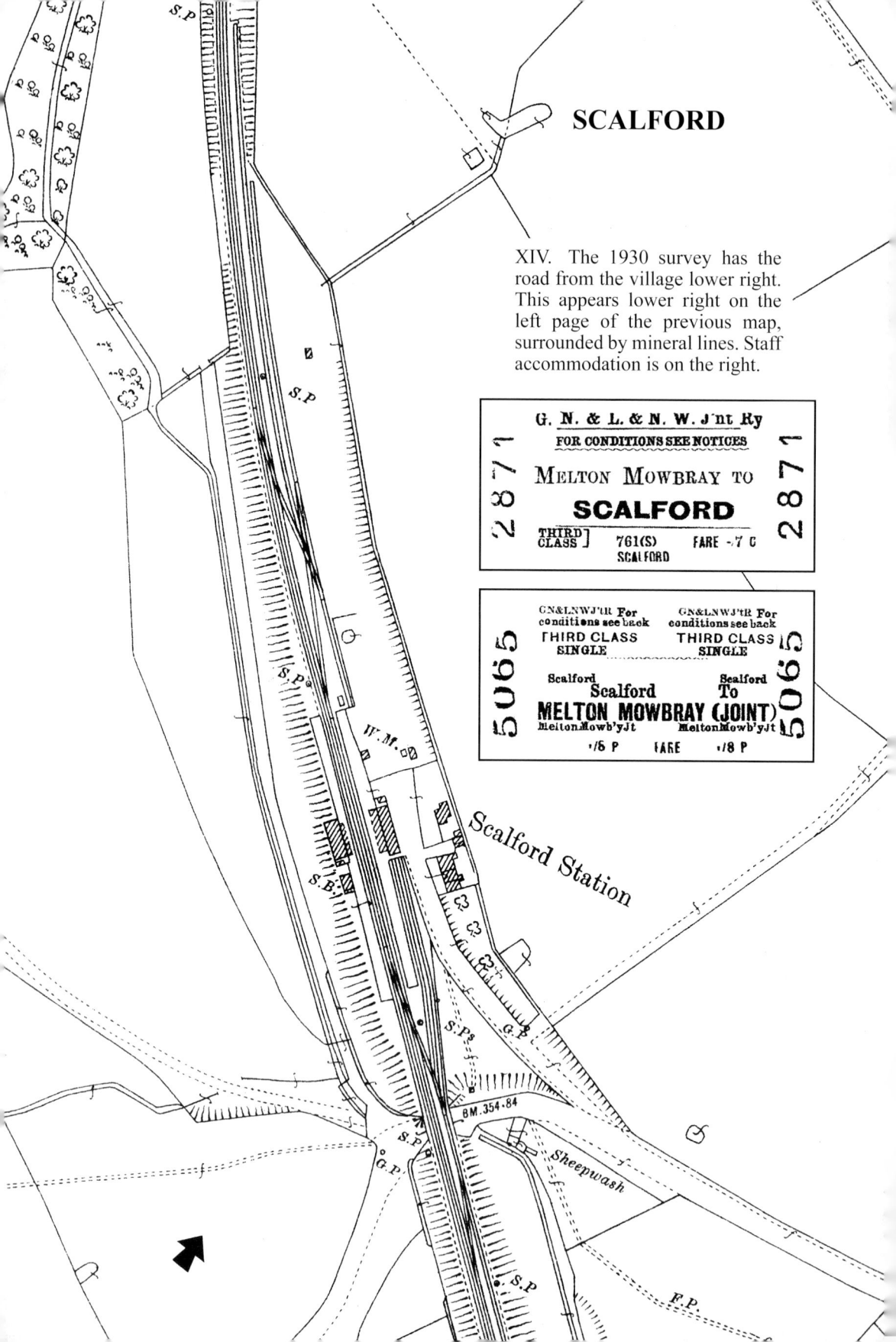

XIV. The 1930 survey has the road from the village lower right. This appears lower right on the left page of the previous map, surrounded by mineral lines. Staff accommodation is on the right.

2871

G. N. & L. & N. W. J'nt Ry
FOR CONDITIONS SEE NOTICES

MELTON MOWBRAY TO
SCALFORD
THIRD CLASS]   761(S)   FARE -.7 C
SCALFORD

2871

5065

GN&LNWJ'tR For conditions see back
THIRD CLASS SINGLE

GN&LNWJ'tR For conditions see back
THIRD CLASS SINGLE

Scalford
Scalford
MELTON MOWBRAY (JOINT)
MeltonMowb'yJt
·/6 P

Scalford
To
Melton Mowb'yJt
·/8 P

FARE

5065

Scalford Station

S.P.

W.M.

S.B.

BM.354·84

Sheepwash

G.P.

S.P.

F.P.

58.   The local population in 1901 was just 631. This view is from 8th July 1955 and includes ex-WD 2-8-0 no. 90075, with an up mineral train. Passengers had to use the crossing in the foreground, but their trains had been withdrawn on 7th December 1953. (Milepost 92½)

59.   It is 21st April 1958 and ore wagons are resting in the bay, probably due to a defect. Local goods service was withdrawn on 4th May 1964. (R.M.Casserley)

60.   Running north on 26th May 1959 is class 8F 2-8-0 no. 48360 hauling iron ore from Waltham Quarry. The goods yard is in the right distance. (J.S.Gilks/M.J.Stretton)

61.   It is 4th April 1959 and shunting is in progress, supervised by the guard leaning on a buffer. No. 48360 has been seen in the previous photograph. The coal supply for the signal box is on the platform. (J.S.Gilks/M.J.Stretton)

62. A Leicester to Mablethorpe express speeds towards the holiday resorts on 27th August 1960, hauled by class B1 4-6-0 no. 61390. The face of the bay platform is evident. (J..S.Gilks/M.J.Stretton)

63. Class B1 4-6-0 no. 61361 runs through with an express from the East Coast on 18th August 1962. The 1879 signal box had a 20-lever frame and was in use until April 1964. All the station building had gone by then. (Colour-Rail.com)

LONG CLAWSON & HOSE

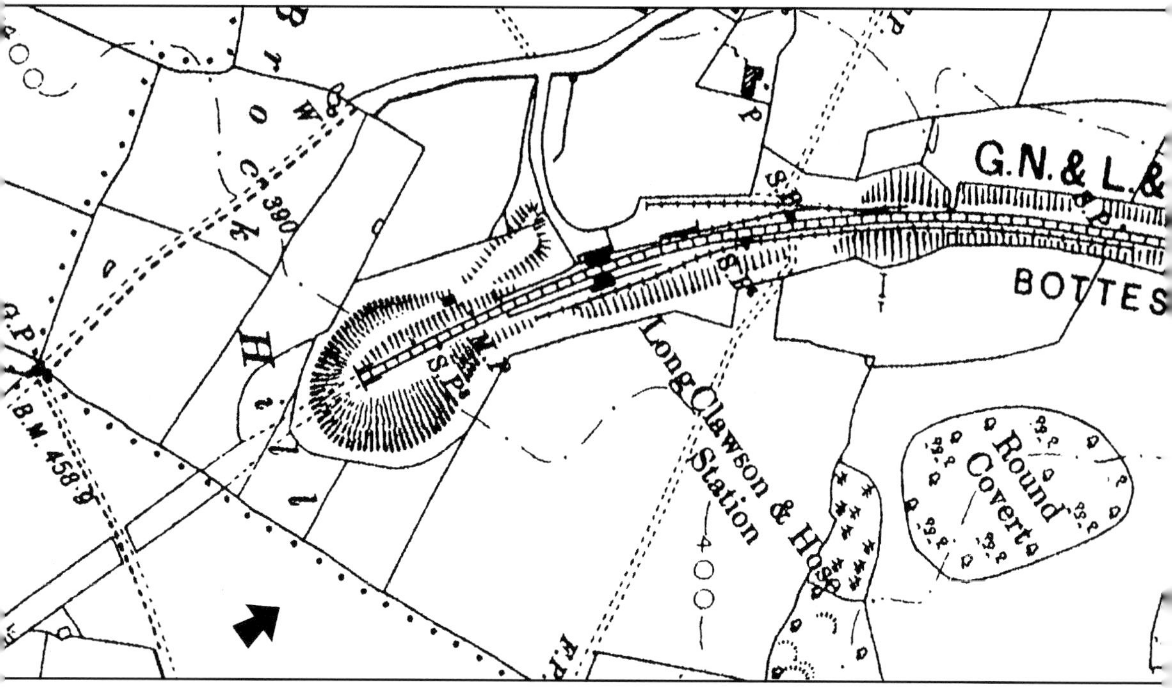

XV. The 1902 edition at 12ins to 1 mile shows little habitation. Long Clawson was four miles distant by road and Hose was 2½. The latter was added to the station name in 1884. The former housed 776 souls in 1901. Lower left is Hose Tunnel, which was 833 yards long.

64.   A view north in 1952 features just two seats. Passenger traffic ceased on 7th December 1953, but goods lasted until 4th May 1964. The 1879 GNR signal box had 24 levers. (Stations UK)

65.   The goods yard is beyond the signal post and the access road is in the woods. The replacement box is seen and it closed in 1953. Shrubs encroach and so the end must be nigh. (Colour-Rail.com)

NORTH OF LONG CLAWSON & HOSE

66.   The box is called Stathern Ironstone Sidings and dates from about 1887. Its 20-lever frame was in use until 20th December 1967. The sidings were on the east side of the running lines and received ore from the Eastwell and Eaton districts. There were two sidings each side of the loading drop. The routes are shown on map XIII in 1951. Many were narrow gauge and there was one rope-worked incline. (Milepost 92½)

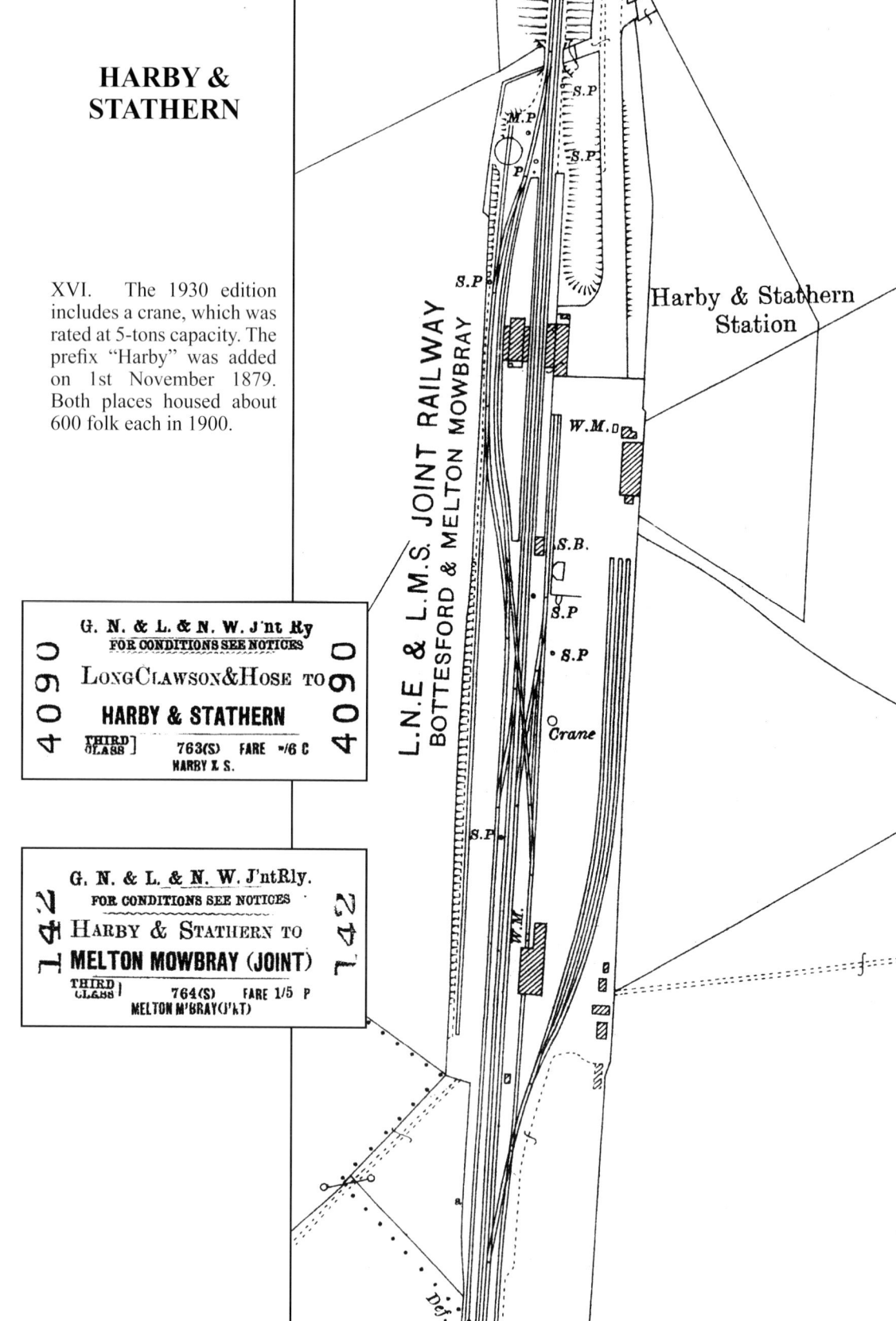

HARBY & STATHERN

XVI. The 1930 edition includes a crane, which was rated at 5-tons capacity. The prefix "Harby" was added on 1st November 1879. Both places housed about 600 folk each in 1900.

S.P.

M.P.

S.P.

P.

S.P.

Harby & Stathern
Station

W.M.D.

S.B.

S.P.

S.P.

Crane

L.N.E & L.M.S. JOINT RAILWAY
BOTTESFORD & MELTON MOWBRAY

S.P.

W.W.

67. A fine postcard includes all four important buildings; only three platforms are shown, the fourth being a bay, which is on the right in the next photo. Passenger service continued until 7th December 1953. (LOSA)

68. A 1949 view north shows that the up building had been replaced, but devoid of shelters. This was a windswept station on the level ground of the Wolds and not ideal as a junction. Trains originated from Newark, Nottingham, Leicester and Market Harborough, but shunting was often necessary to provide connections. (Stations UK)

69.   "The Leicestershire Woldsman" railtour was hauled by class 4 4-6-0 no. 75059 on 19th June 1960. At the rear was another class 4. Operated by the Railway Enthusiasts Club, the train started at Leicester London Road and terminated at Belgrave Road. (J.S.Gilks/M.J.Stretton)

70.   Seen on 22nd April 1961 is Stathern Station Box. It never received the prefix "Harby". Class 8F 2-8-0 no. 48211 is working ironstone empties, southwards. The 1879 box had 35 levers and was worked until 12 February 1968, although the goods yard closed on 7th December 1964. (Milepost 92½)

NORTH OF HARBY & STATHERN

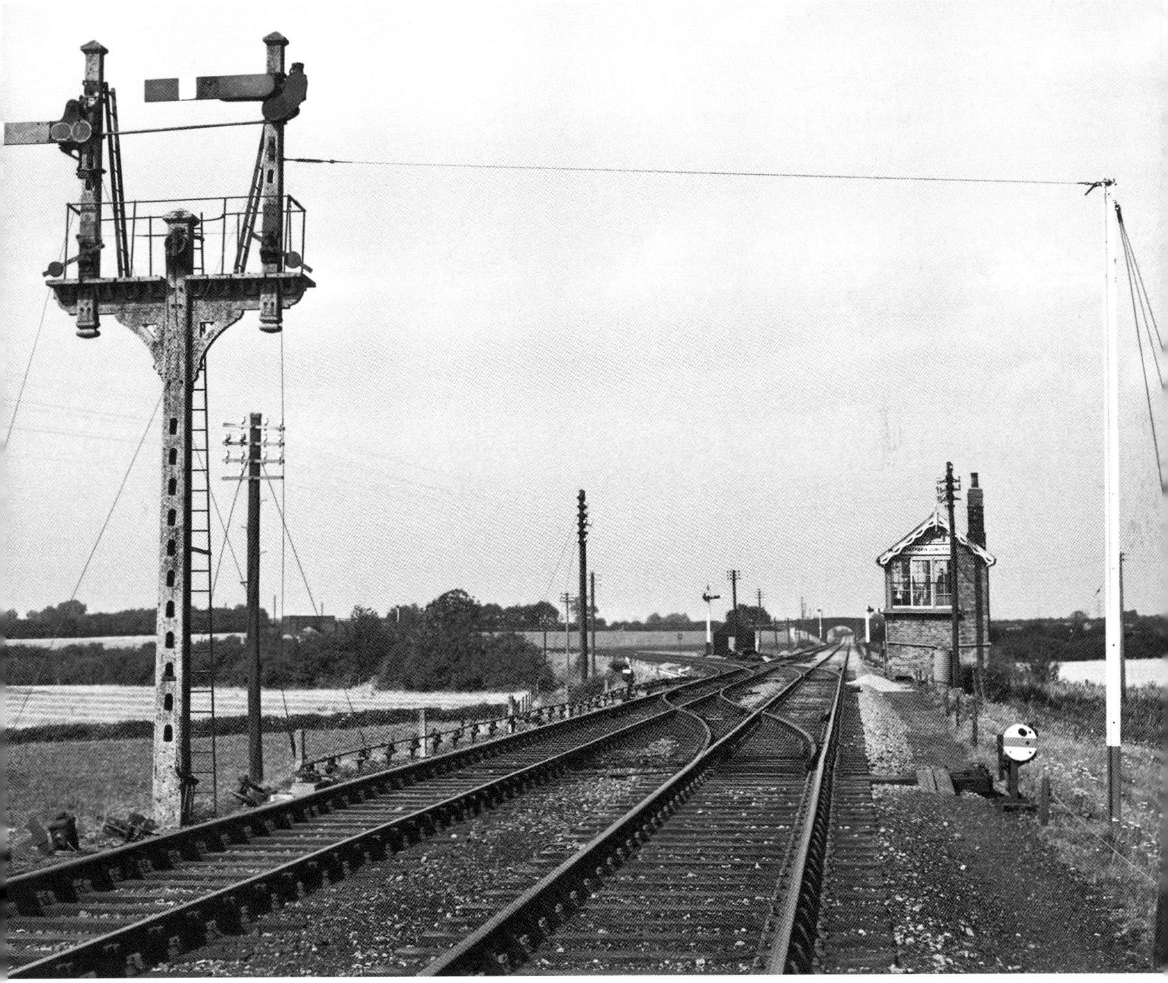

71. Stathern Junction appears on maps I and XIII. Here we look north on 8th September 1962 and the route to Barnstone diverges left. We will look at that short connection, before continuing north. This 1879 box had 20 levers and was in use until 24th May 1964.
(T.G.Hepburn/Rail Archive Stephenson)

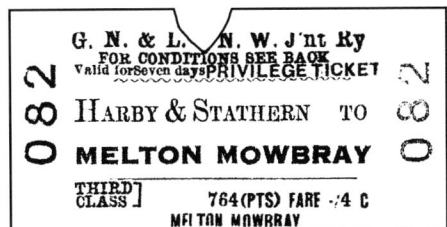

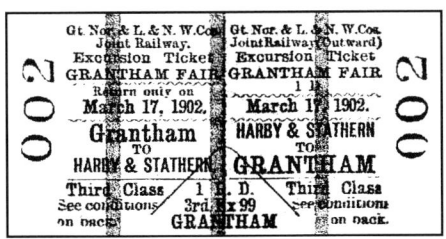

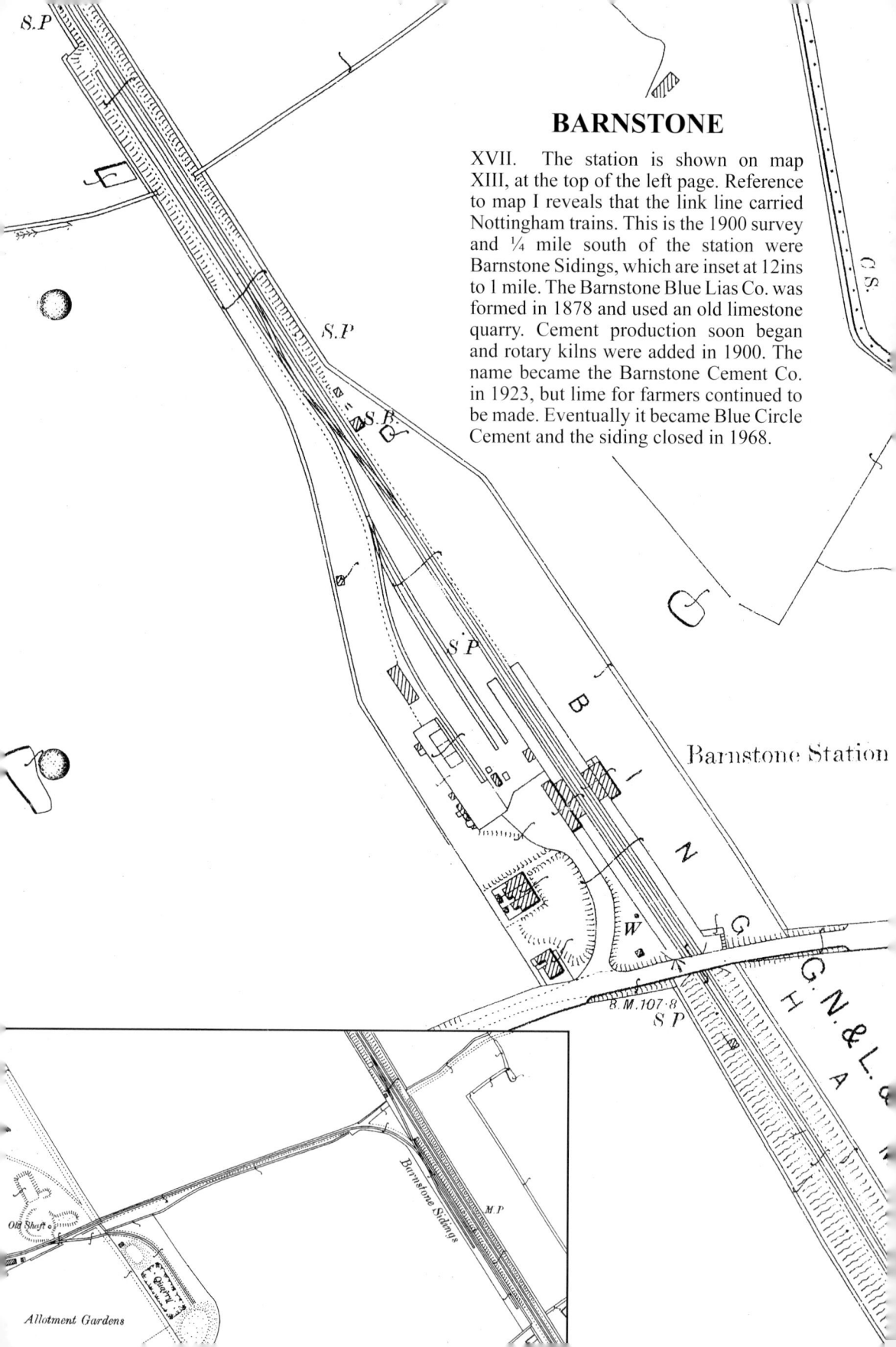

BARNSTONE

XVII.   The station is shown on map XIII, at the top of the left page. Reference to map I reveals that the link line carried Nottingham trains. This is the 1900 survey and ¼ mile south of the station were Barnstone Sidings, which are inset at 12ins to 1 mile. The Barnstone Blue Lias Co. was formed in 1878 and used an old limestone quarry. Cement production soon began and rotary kilns were added in 1900. The name became the Barnstone Cement Co. in 1923, but lime for farmers continued to be made. Eventually it became Blue Circle Cement and the siding closed in 1968.

Barnstone Station

Allotment Gardens

72. The station opened on 30th June 1879 for goods and 1st September 1879 for passengers. Closure to the latter came on 7th December 1953 and the former on 10th September 1962. The yard is on the left. The 22-lever signal box was in use until 9th September 1962. (J.Langford coll.)

73. Class 2P 4-4-0 no. 40683 arrives with a Nottingham Victoria to Northampton service on 4th August 1953. The photo was taken from the Barnstone to Granby Lane bridge. (T.G.Hepburn/Rail Archive Stephenson)

BINGHAM ROAD

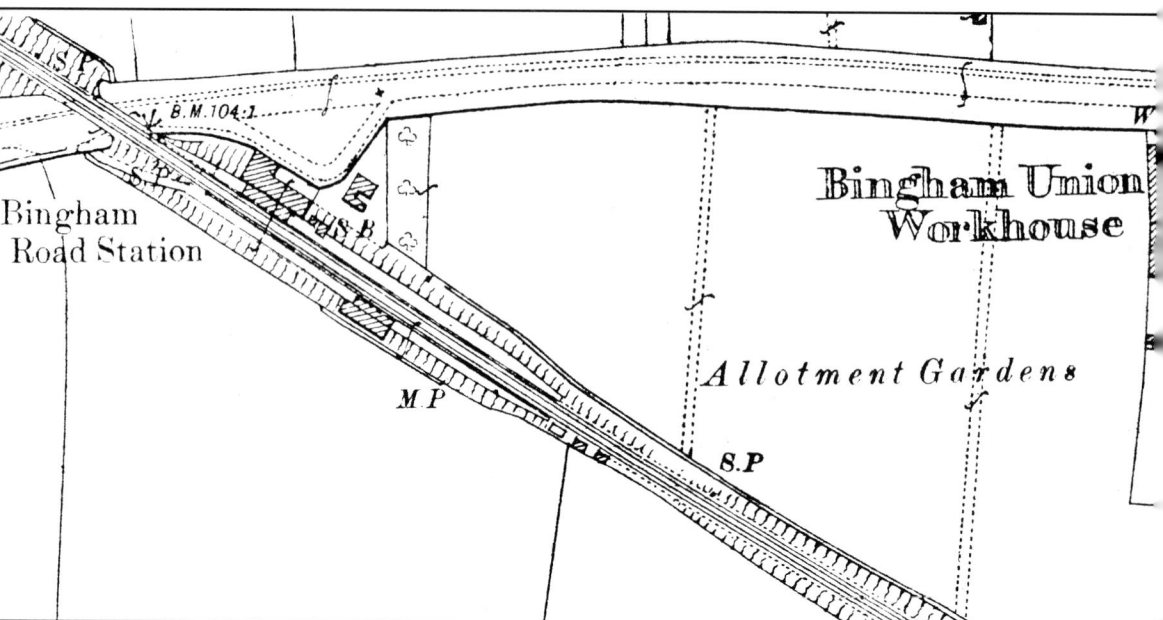

XVIII.   The 1900 map features the Nottingham to Grantham road, which became the A52 in 1919. The Workhouse is at the west end of the village of Bingham and was a home for the unemployed of a union of parishes.

74.   This eastward view has the footway entrance to the down platform on the right and the approach road beyond the bridge. Bingham's main station is illustrated in pictures 42 to 47 in our *Nottingham to Boston* album and Saxondale Junction is shown in no. 41. (LOSA)

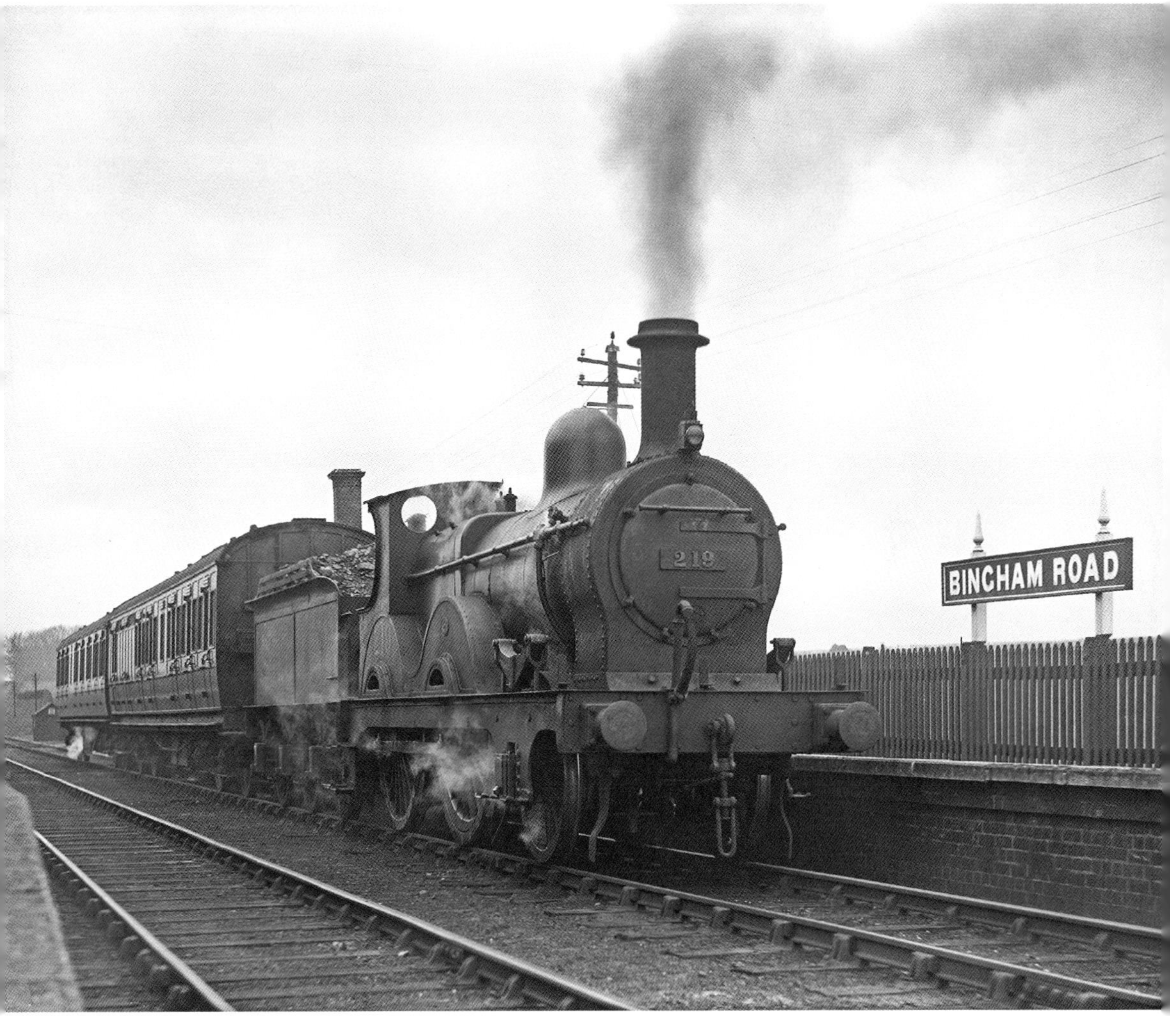

75. Ex-MR class 1P 2-4-0 no. 219 calls with a Nottingham London Road service in about 1935. Passenger service was withdrawn here on 2nd July 1951. The booking office contained a lever frame near its bay window until 1918. (T.G.Hepburn/Rail Archive Stephenson)

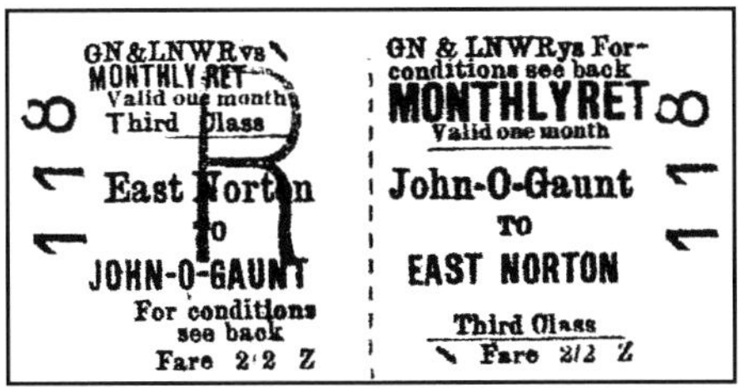

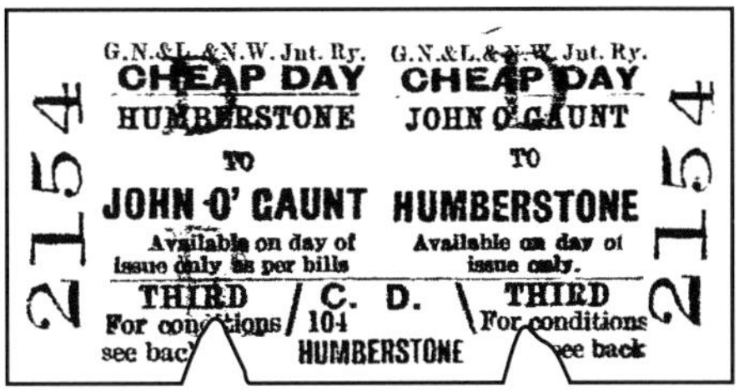

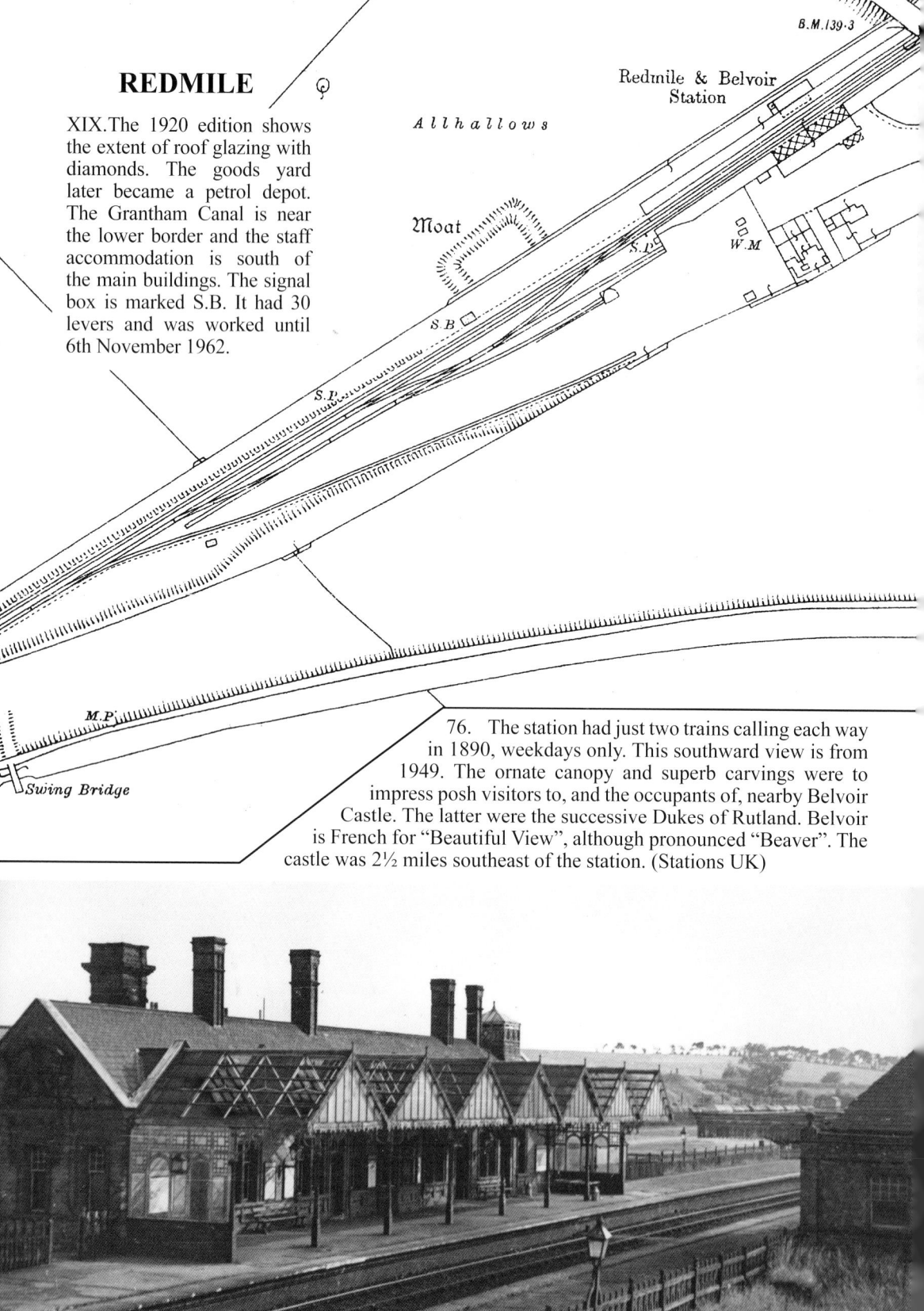

REDMILE

XIX. The 1920 edition shows the extent of roof glazing with diamonds. The goods yard later became a petrol depot. The Grantham Canal is near the lower border and the staff accommodation is south of the main buildings. The signal box is marked S.B. It had 30 levers and was worked until 6th November 1962.

Allhallows

Moat

Redmile & Belvoir Station

B.M.139·3

S.D.

W.M.

S.B.

S.D.

M.P.

Swing Bridge

76.   The station had just two trains calling each way in 1890, weekdays only. This southward view is from 1949. The ornate canopy and superb carvings were to impress posh visitors to, and the occupants of, nearby Belvoir Castle. The latter were the successive Dukes of Rutland. Belvoir is French for "Beautiful View", although pronounced "Beaver". The castle was 2½ miles southeast of the station. (Stations UK)

77. The June 1951 timetable showed just an 8.12am to Grantham and a 7.56pm to Leicester, weekdays only. Goods and passenger services ceased on 7th December 1953. A Leicester to Skegness service speeds through, but no other details were kept. (M.J.Stretton coll.)

78. There were private waiting rooms for the Dukes and their company, but sadly all were demolished. The 7.10pm Grantham to Leicester Belgrave Road is seen on 19th June 1950, hauled by class J6 0-6-0 no. 64206. (T.G.Hepburn/Rail Archive Stephenson)

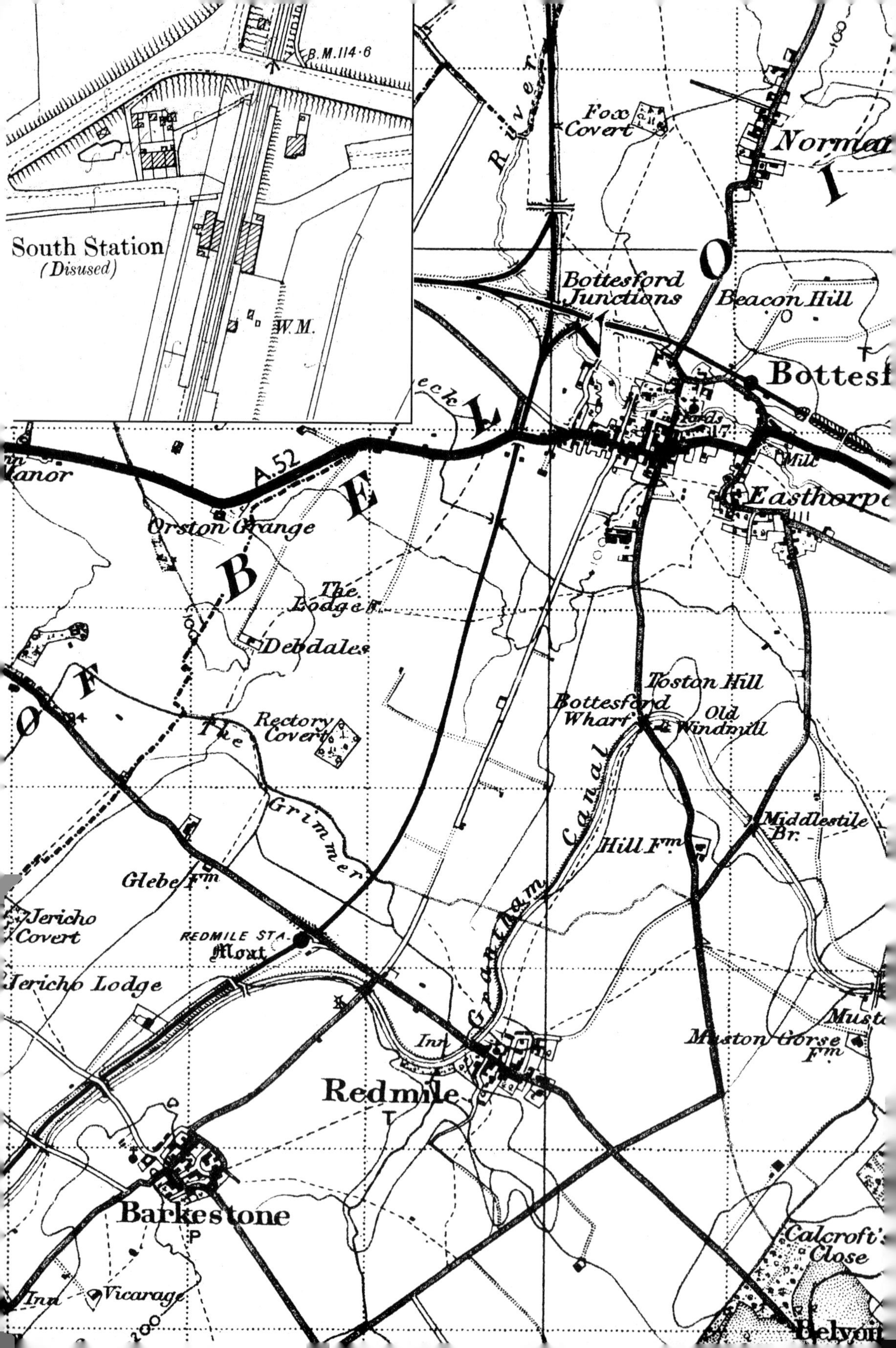

South Station
(Disused)

B.M.114·6

W.M.

River

Fox
Covert

Norma

Bottesford
Junctions

Beacon Hill

O

I

Bottesf

L

A.52

E

Mill

Easthorpe

Manor

Orston Grange

B

The
Lodge

Debdales

Toston Hill

Bottesford
Wharf

Old
Windmill

O

F

The

Rectory
Covert

Middlestile
Br.

Hill Fm

Grimmer

Glebe Fm

Jericho
Covert

REDMILE STA.

Moat

Jericho Lodge

Inn

Muston Gorse
Fm

Must

Redmile

Barkestone

Calcroft's
Close

Inn

Vicarage

Belvoi

NORTH OF REDMILE

← XX. The 1947 edition at 2ins to 1 mile has Redmile lower centre. The road to Belvoir Castle passes through it. Inset is an extract from the 1900 edition. This shows Bottesford South station, which had closed on 1st May 1882. The 1850 station on the east-west route is still open and can be seen in pictures nos 61 to 70 in our *Nottingham to Boston* album. The junction can be seen in pictures 59 and 60. Lower right is a tramway between the castle and the canal. South station was demolished, but the staff dwellings remained standing. The west-south curve is shown as single track. It was in use in 1879-90 and it was reopened for mineral traffic from 9th January 1962 until 12th December 1970.

2JLY46
G.N. and L. & N.W. Joint Ry
Issued subject to the conditions contained in the Time Bills & Notices of the GN.&L&NW.Ry Cos
REDMILE TO
GREAT DALBY
THIRD CLASS 767 (S) FARE 1 11
GREAT DALBY
796

010
Gt. Nor. & L. & N. W. Cos. Joint Railway.
Excursion Ticket
GRANTHAM FAIR
Return only on
March 17, 1902.
Grantham TO REDMILE & BELVOIR
Third Class 1 D.
See conditions on back.

Gt. Nor. & L. & N. W. Cos. Joint Railway (Outward)
Excursion Ticket
GRANTHAM FAIR 1 D.
March 17. 1902.
REDMILE & BELVOIR TO GRANTHAM
Third Class
See conditions on back.
3rd E 96
GRANTHAM
010

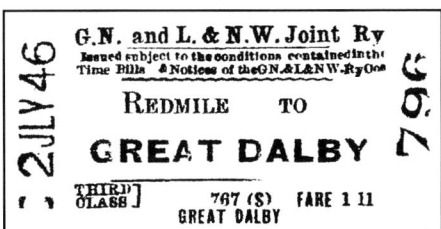

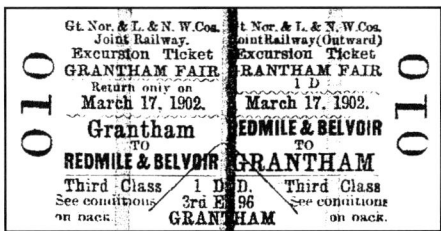

79. Class B1 4-6-0 no. 61248 *Geoffrey Gibbs* passes Bottesford South Junction and heads for the East Junction with a Leicester Belgrave Road to Skegness train in about 1962. North Junction Box had 20 levers and was in use until 18th February 1962. In the foreground is a trolley berth for the track gang. (T.G.Hepburn/Rail Archive Stephenson)

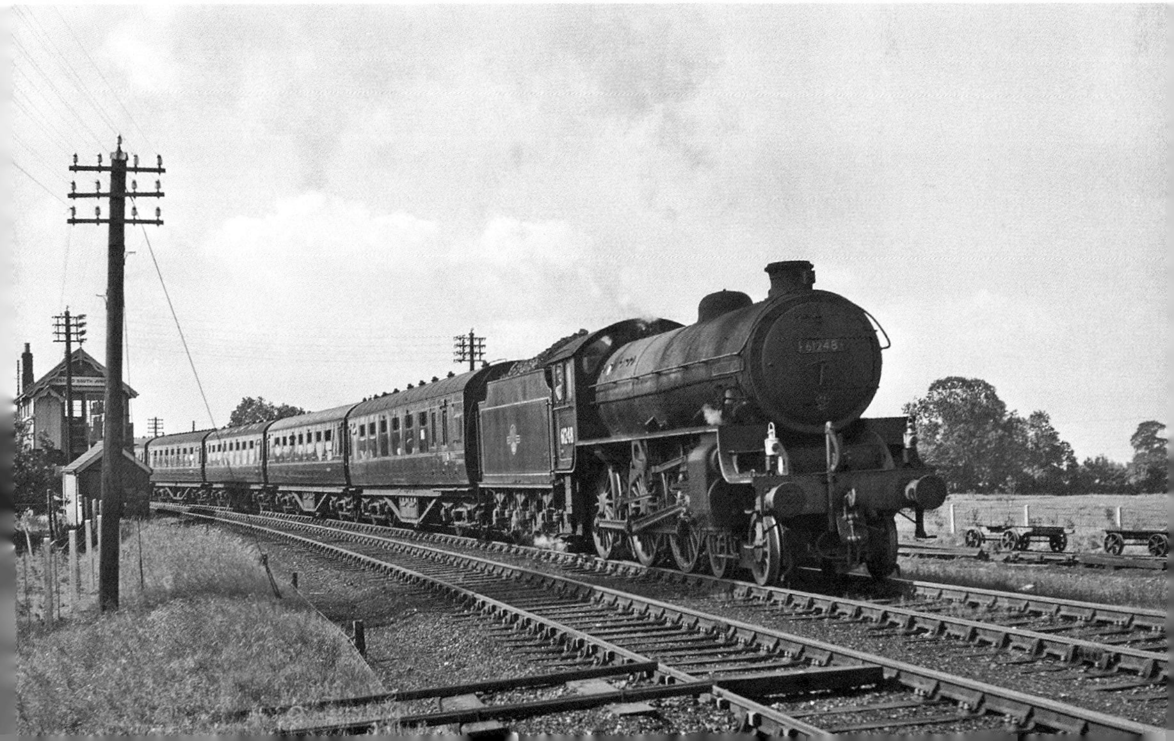

80.   We see Bottesford South Junction after track lifting towards the West Junction, in the early 1970s. The north-south link was lost in 1962. The 1879 box had 30 levers and closed on 9th September 1962. Bottesford West Junction Box closed on 27th November 2015, along with Bingham Box, to the west of it. (T.G.Hepburn/Rail Archive Stephenson)

SOUTH OF COTHAM

81.   Class J6 0-6-0 no. 64269 is seen near Cotham with a Newark to Nottingham train in around 1950. In addition to the gypsum sidings north of the station, there were connections to Nottinghamshire Gypsum Products Ltd and Bellrock Gypsum Industries Ltd south of it, on the east side of the running line. (T.G.Hepburn/Rail Archive Stephenson)

COTHAM

XXI.   The 1930 edition includes the staff cottages, west of the track. Passenger service ceased early: 11th September 1939. This was a wartime economy measure, as was the previous closure from 2nd April 1917 to 1st April 1919.

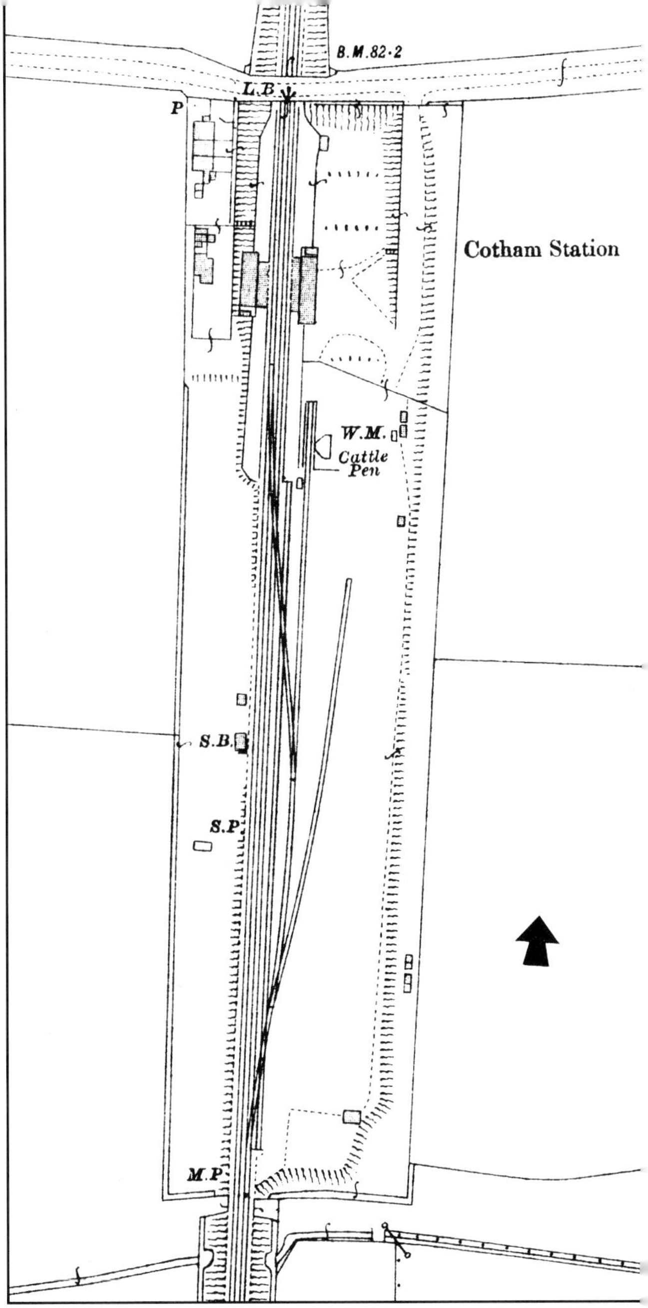

Cotham Station

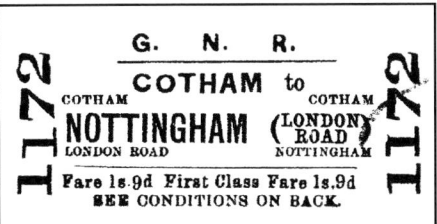

82. The signal box is facing the goods yard, which closed on 3rd February 1964. The 25-lever box was in use until 18th February 1962. The station had opened in the year after the line; on 14th April 1879. The population was 113 in 1901. The photo is from 1954. (Stations UK)

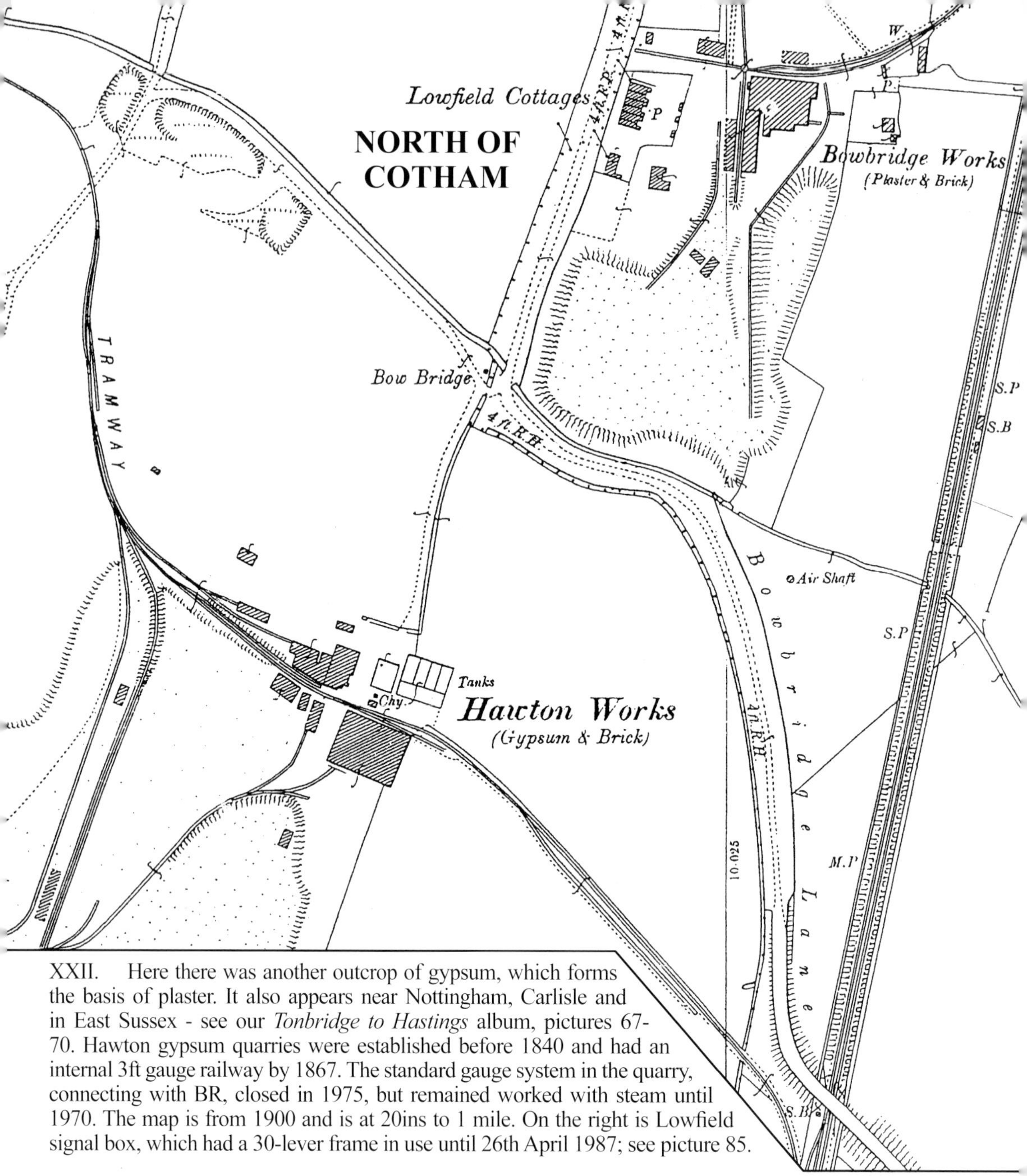

NORTH OF COTHAM

Lowfield Cottages

Bowbridge Works
(*Plaster & Brick*)

TRAMWAY

Bow Bridge

Air Shaft

Tanks
Hawton Works
(*Gypsum & Brick*)

XXII.   Here there was another outcrop of gypsum, which forms the basis of plaster. It also appears near Nottingham, Carlisle and in East Sussex - see our *Tonbridge to Hastings* album, pictures 67-70. Hawton gypsum quarries were established before 1840 and had an internal 3ft gauge railway by 1867. The standard gauge system in the quarry, connecting with BR, closed in 1975, but remained worked with steam until 1970. The map is from 1900 and is at 20ins to 1 mile. On the right is Lowfield signal box, which had a 30-lever frame in use until 26th April 1987; see picture 85.

83. The last working steam locomotive at Hawton Gypsum Works was this 1947 Sentinel vertical boilered geared locomotive *St. Monans*, seen in action on 2nd May 1970. It was replaced by a diesel locomotive the following year but was preserved. Much plaster had been despatched on the River Trent. Steam arrived in 1901 and soon replaced horses on the tramways. (J.A.Peden/IRS coll.)

84. Seen awaiting the scrap man in 1954 was this 1882 Fletcher Jennings 0-4-0T. Earlier, a 3-foot gauge system had been in use. Some sections were dual gauge for a time. The output had often been 250 tons per day, all dug by hand. (A.Neale coll.)

85. The line from Bottesford West Junction to Newark South Junction remained open for freight until 1987. In later years it was used mainly by oil trains between Immingham and the Total oil terminal at Colwick (Rectory Junction). No. 56085 pauses for token exchange at Lowfield box, with the 09.54 Rectory Junction to Immingham empty tank train, on 31st July 1984. BR was able to close the Bottesford to Newark line with relatively little adverse impact. The oil trains were diverted via Nottingham in the outward direction and via Grantham on the return journey. The former freight line was converted into a pleasant and useful cycle track and footpath. (P.D.Shannon)

SOUTH OF NEWARK

86. Several substantial engineering businesses were developed on the outskirts of Newark and much agricultural equipment was produced. In the background in October 1933 is Worthington-Simpson's factory and the train is carrying its output of petrol refinery pumps, destined for Iraq. It is hauled by a class J3 0-6-0.
(Newark Civil War Centre/ Newark Museum)

87. Newark Junction is lower right on the next map and is where our route joins the main line from Grantham. It had 45 levers and was in use from 1878 until 1931.
(Newark Civil War Centre/ Newark Museum)

NEWARK NORTHGATE

NEWARK

Bottom Lock
Chemical Manure Works

RIVER TRENT

NEWARK BRANCH

Weir

Malthouses

King's Sconce (Site of)

Malthouses

Strawberry Hall

Tank

Football Ground

Malthouses
Roman Coins &c found

Spital Row

P.H.

Wellington Foundry

Station

Goods Shed Wharf

Malthouses

Chap.

Sch.

Ch.

Sch.

Malthouses

Sta.

Tank

Malthouses

Trent Works

Malthouse

Meth. Chap.

Trent Bridge

Nursery

Newark Junction

Engine Shed

Hatton House

Newark Boiler Works

Site Royalist

Beaconhill

XXIII.   This is the 1902 edition at 5ins to 1 mile. The next two maps give more detail, as they are five times larger. The station on the left is Newark Castle and is on the MR, which runs northeast to Lincoln and crosses over the GNR to Doncaster, on the level. The curved connection between the two straight routes was for freight and was in use from 1869 to 1973. A south to east connection between the two straight routes was added in 1965. Details can be found in our *Nottingham to Lincoln* album.

Malthouses

Pinfold

B.M.42·3

XXIVa. The 1900 survey
continues south on the next
extract, but all the passenger
facilities are on this one.

Strawberry Hall

S.B. Tank

S.P

LINCOLN STREET

B.M.41·9   B.M.43·5

Goods Shed

S.P

B.M.411

S.P

N E

STRANCE STREET

P

P

P

P

P

Railway Hotel
(P.H.) P

Station

B.M.407

B.M.44

B.M.43·1

P

P

Goods Shed

M.P

S.P⁵

althouse

B.M.41

Goods Shed

P

Cattle
Pen

S.P

B.M.40·4

S.P

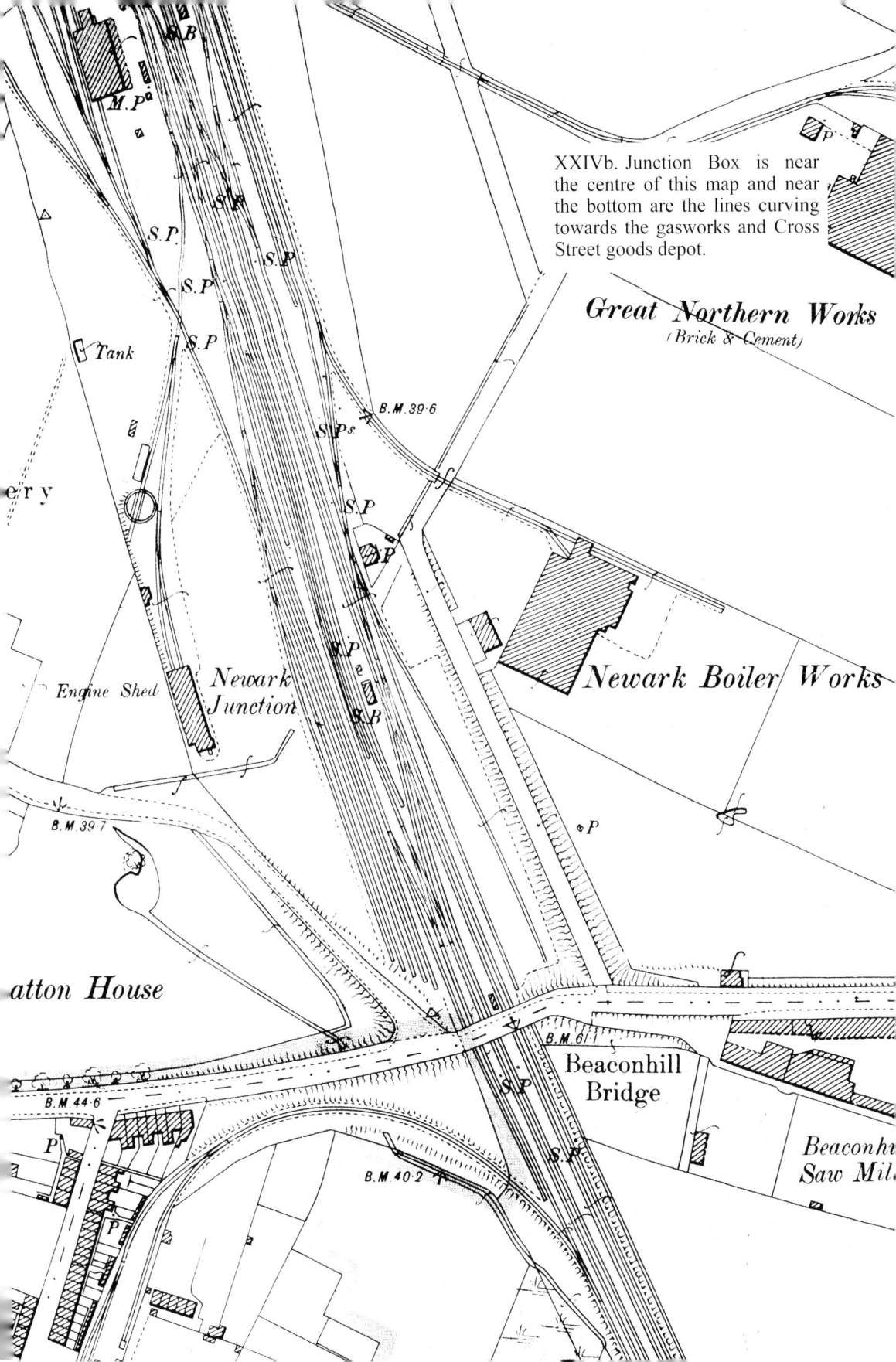

M.B

M.P

S.P

S.P

S.P

S.P

S.P

△

Tank

er y

XXIVb. Junction Box is near the centre of this map and near the bottom are the lines curving towards the gasworks and Cross Street goods depot.

Great Northern Works
(Brick & Cement)

B.M.39·6

S.Ps

S.P

S.P

P

Engine Shed

Newark Junction

P

B

Newark Boiler Works

B.M.39·7

P

atton House

B.M.6

Beaconhill Bridge

S.P

Beaconh
Saw Mil

B.M.44·6

P

P

P

B.M.40·2

S.P

88. A poor quality photograph of a Boer War military ceremony on 22nd October 1901 is included as it shows the outline of the goods shed, which was of great importance to the town. It was demolished in 1983, to increase provision for car parking.
(Newark Civil War Centre/Newark Museum)

Nottinghamshire Guardian -
Thursday, 25th October 1860.

89. The main building of 1881 is featured, together with the 1883 footbridge, Lincoln Road bridge was built in the distance in 1936 and it replaced a level crossing. (P.Laming coll.)

TERRIFIC EXPLOSION IN THE GREAT NORTHERN RAILWAY STATION

•

On Tuesday morning a fearful explosion took place in the Newark station yard of the Great Northern Railway, just as the 7·44 am train was about starting north. The passengers had taken their seats, and the whistle had sounded, when, in a moment, a most alarming explosion took place, with a report that might be heard for miles distant. The brass dome on the top of the boiler, with which the safety valve is connected, was blown direct in the air, a height of 30 or 40 yards, and the main part of it fell through the roof of the platform on the same side of the station yard, thirty yards or so from the place where the engine was standing... Providently, no one was injured.

90.   South Box was completed by the LNER in 1931 and its 105-lever frame was in use until 3rd February 1980. The use of the suffix NORTHGATE began in 1950, but as two words periodically. (Newark Civil War Centre/Newark Museum)

91.   The down side is seen in the days of mailbags on passenger trains. A new footbridge, complete with lifts, arrived in 2007. The down bay is in the distance, but it did not have the protection seen in the next picture. It had been used by trains on our route. (Newark Civil War Centre/Newark Museum)

92. The up bay platform was well protected from the elements and Nottingham passengers were the beneficiaries. However, when trains began running to and from Lincoln on the new connection, the buildings were cleared and a through platform, numbered 3, was created. (Newark Civil War Centre/Newark Museum)

93. The massive granary is top left on map XXIVb. Behind the camera was the engine shed, which closed on 31st January 1959. (Newark Civil War Centre/Newark Museum)

2. Leicester Belgrave Road Branch
LOWESBY

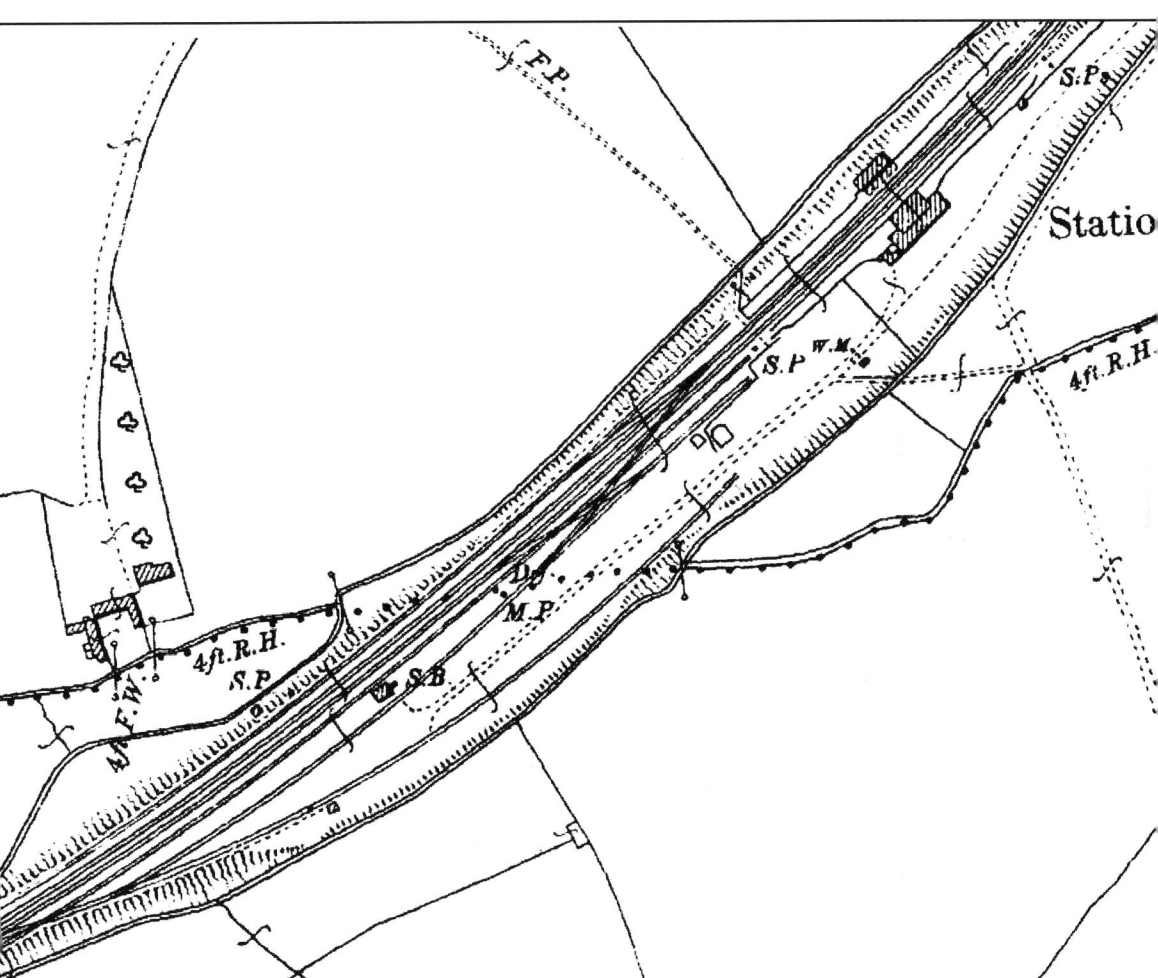

XXV. The 1903 survey has a stream running diagonally under the goods yard, which has unusually clearly marked cart tracks. Lowesby Hall and its village of 107 souls, was almost one mile northwest of the station.

**For recent views and other old ones,
please see our** *Peterborough to Newark* **and**
Newark to Doncaster **albums.**

94. A 1930s view southwest includes a Somersault signal and Summer smart suiting of the era. Also evident is the staff crossing and an unextinguished lamp. In the distance is the 31-lever signal box, which closed on 7th December 1953, along with the goods yard. (Stations UK)

95. These two coaches were on three bogies and had two lavatories, each having white windows. Class J11 0-6-0 no. 64375 is showing its Eastern Region number acquired in 1948. (N.Stead/M.J.Stretton)

96. We look east on 22nd August 1953, the year in which the local public service was withdrawn. It had offered three trains each way, but weekdays only. The station name was often devoid of a W until 1916. The site is now part of a farm. (H.C.Casserley)

97. It is August 1960 and one of the holiday trains is returning to Leicester. There was the 1.52pm from Mablethorpe on Saturdays or the 7.20pm from Skegness on Sundays, but neither stopped here, nor at the next two stations. (F.Cassell/M.J.Stretton)

INGARSBY

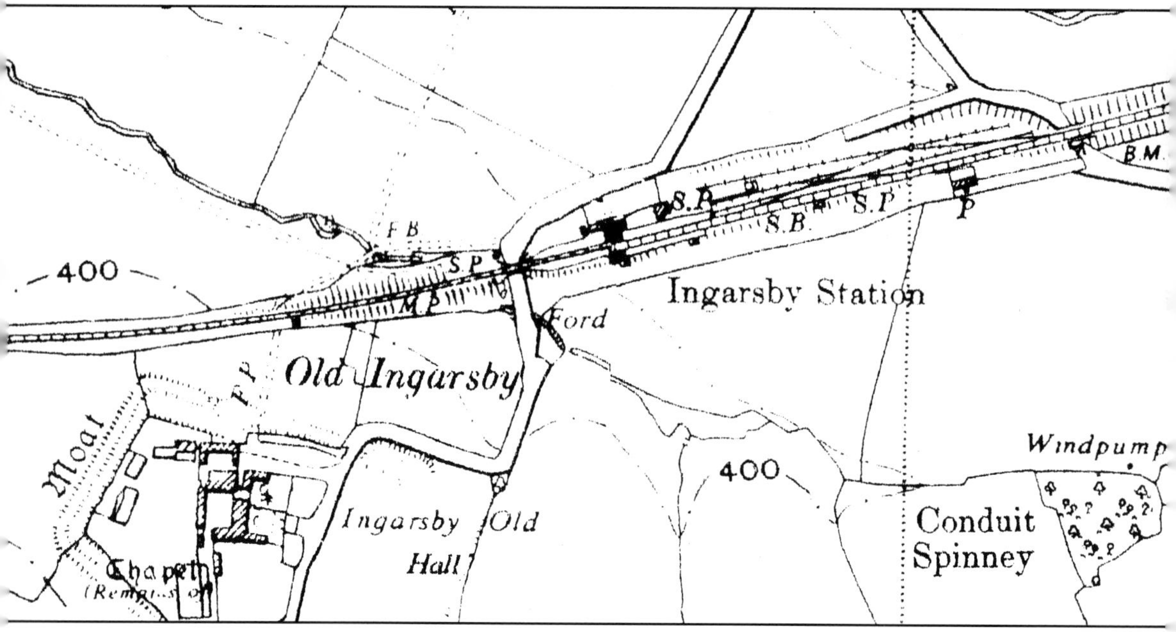

XXVI.   The 1951 edition is shown at 12ins to 1 mile. The name was INGERSBY until 1939.

98.   An early postcard includes stock in the goods yard. This was in use until 5th March 1951. Milk churns are evident, but diminished from the railway scene in the 1930s. (LOSA)

99. A sharp eastward view includes the 26-lever signal box, which lasted in use until local passenger trains ceased on 7th December 1953. (M.J.Stretton coll.)

100. Class B1 4-6-0 no. 61325 is speeding east on 5th August 1962, hauling many buckets and spades for use on East Coast beaches. No such trains called here. (Colour-Rail.com)

THURNBY & SCRAPTOFT

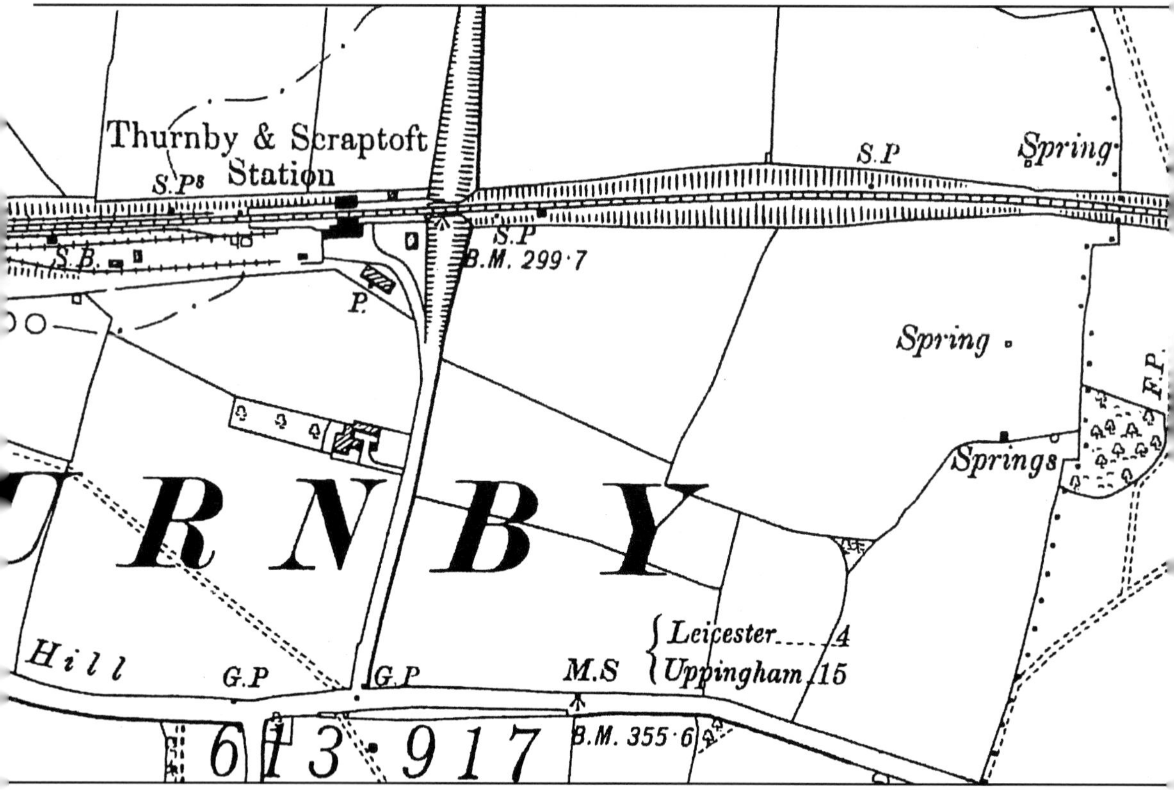

XXVII. The 1929 revision is at 12ins to 1 mile and shows that neither village was close to the station. Thurnby housed 234 in 1901 and Scraptoft 116.

101. A train arrives from the east in the postcard view from around 1900. The crossover gave access from this side to the goods yard. (M.J.Stretton coll.)

102.   The platforms were all on columns to minimise the weight on made-up ground. The down siding is in the background, but we have no details of the rescue operation in progress. (SLS coll.)

103.   Class J11 0-6-0 no. 64301 leaves with the 2.0pm from Grantham, which had connected there with the down "The Flying Scotsman", the 10.0am from Kings Cross. The date is 9th August 1950. (A.Ford/M.J.Stretton)

104.   A 1952 eastward panorama includes the bridge over the lane to Scraptoft, which is one mile to the north. Regular passenger service ceased here on 7th December 1953. (Stations UK)

105.   Left is the signal box, which had 33 levers and remained in use until 31st May 1964. Passing in August 1962 is a holiday express. No. 61142 was a class B1 4-6-0, a type introduced by the LNER in 1942. (A.Ford/M.J.Stretton)

HUMBERSTONE

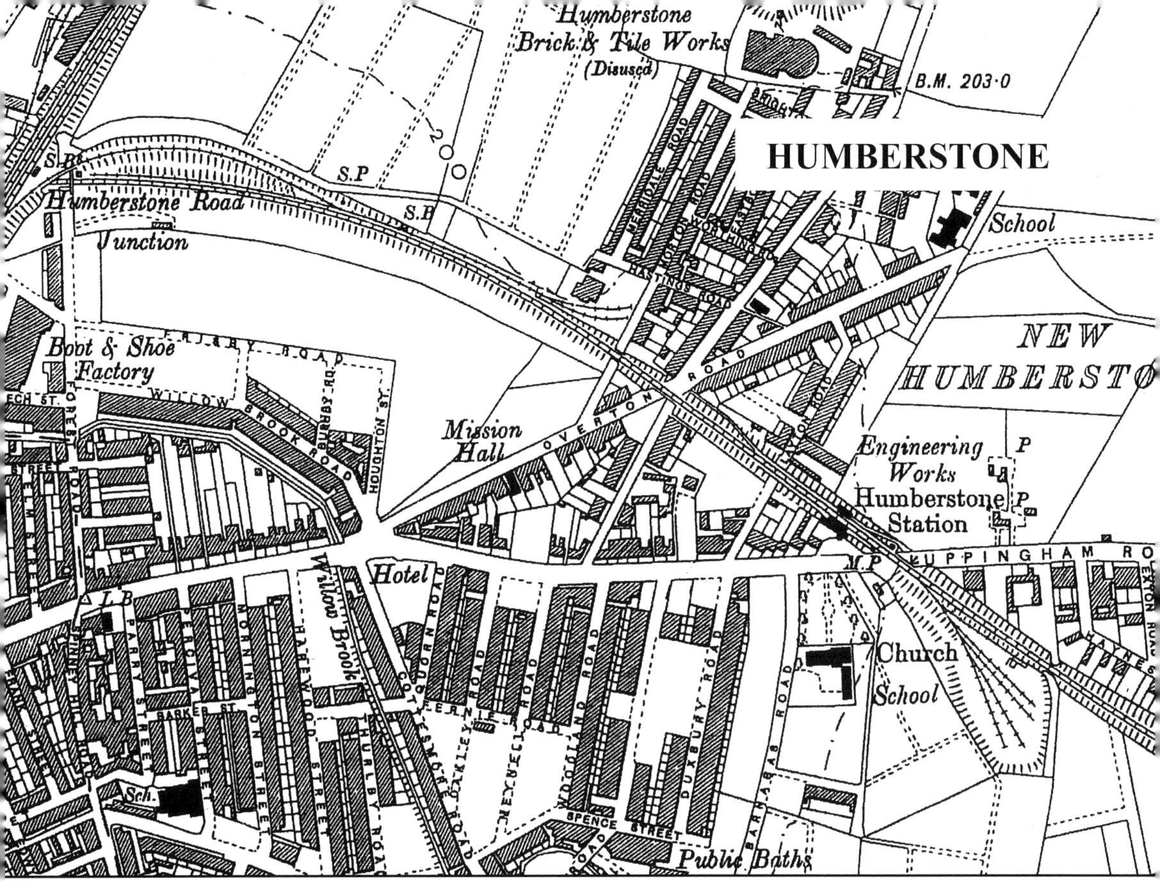

NEW HUMBERSTO

XXVIII.   The 1902 edition is shown at 9ins to 1 mile, with the station and its yard on the right. The junction on the left is explained in caption 110. The local passenger service was withdrawn on 7th December 1953, but workmens trains continued until 26th April 1957. The goods yard closed on 1st May 1967.

106.   The postcard view of the south elevation includes two of Leicester's trams. Its system operated electrically from 18th May 1904 until 9th November 1949. (P.Laming coll.)

107.   The location of the signal box in relation to the bridge is revealed in the previous picture also. This view is from about 1959 and it includes some of the 15 levers. It was worked as a ground frame from 1957 until closure on 1st June 1964. (Milepost 92½)

108.   The 13.50 from Skegness arrives on 6th August 1960, headed by class B1 4-6-0 no. 61163. There are fire buckets at both ends of the foot crossing, as most of the surroundings are made of timber. (F.Cassell/M.J.Stretton)

109. This is the signalman's view on Bank Holiday Monday, 7th August 1961. Class B1 no. 61142 brings in the 9.20am from Belgrave Road and crowds bound for Skegness are ready to board. Such trains continued for another year. (H.Gamble/M.J.Stretton)

WEST OF HUMBERSTONE

110. The former MR passes over our route on the approach to its terminus at Belgrave Road. The photo is from June 1961 and features the 14-levered box, which closed on 31st May 1964. There was a curve linking the two routes briefly in 1888. It was removed unused in 1908. It was relaid and used from 1st June 1964 to 1st January 1969. The route west of Humberstone was closed almost entirely on 1st May 1967 and east thereof on 1st June 1964. Between the bridges is Humberstone Road Box. (B.Hilton/M.J.Stretton)

LEICESTER BELGRAVE ROAD

XXIX.   Our route is on the right and overlaps the previous map. On it can be seen the junction layout more clearly. The Belgrave Road terminal buildings are top left; black indicates passengers and grey is for goods. The same applies to the MR station, lower left, but the circular ones are engine sheds. These structures are illustrated in our *Wellingborough to Leicester* and *Leicester to Burton* albums. Further west was the GCR route, which is featured in *Rugby to Loughborough*. The engine shed is at the east end of the yard and housed a few small locomotives until June 1955. Subsequently, all engines had to come from Colwick Shed, east of Nottingham.

111.   The fine styling of the west elevation is presented on this postcard, together with parts of the two train shed roofs. The gable ends of the goods shed roofs are on the left. (P.Laming coll.)

112.   A closer look in 1952 and one is offered the service of the POSTAL TELEGRAPH OFFICE. From here one could despatch personal telegrams. The railways pioneered the use of lineside wires. The Vauxhall car was easy to identify, as the two bright strips on the bonnet formed a V, when seen from an elevated position. (R.M.Casserley)

113. It is 11th April 1952 and class J6 0-6-0 no. 64249 simmers on the left, as nos 64200 and 64257 wait to pull away with a heavy train to Skegness. They are also class J6. On the right is stored stock, including one coach in "blood and custard" livery. (A.Ford/M.J.Stretton)

MARKET HARBORO', LEICESTER, NOTTINGHAM, and GRANTHAM.—L. & N. E. and L. M. & S.

Miles	Down. Week Days only.	mrn	mrn	mrn	mrn	mrn	aft	mrn		aft	aft		aft	aft	aft	aft		aft	aft		
	363 London (Euston) .... dep.	....	....	5 0	....	6 45	....	9 30	....	....	....	....	1215	....	....	....	Through Carriage, London (Euston) to Melton Mowbray.	4 15	....	....	....
	363 Northampton (Castle) "	....	....	6 55	....	9 10	....	1255	....	....	....	....	2 50	4 20	....	....		6 0	....	....	....
—	Market Harboro' .... dep.	....	....	7 44	....	9 59	....	1 55	....	....	....	....	3 50	5 20	....	....		6 50	....	....	....
6¾	Hallaton	....	....	7 56	....	10 12	....	2 8	....	....	....	....	4 3	5 33	....	....		7 4	....	....	....
9	East Norton	....	....	8 2	....	10 18	....	2 16	....	....	....	....	4 9	5 45	....	....		7 11	....	....	....
14	Tilton .... arr.	....	....	8 9	....	10 26	....	2 24	....	....	....	....	4 17	5 53	....	....		7 19	....	....	....
	Tilton dep.		....	8 10	....	10 27	....	2 25	....	....	....	....	4 18	5 54	....	....		7 20	....	....	....
—	Mls Leicester (Belgr'veRd) dep.	Wednesdays only.	7 5	....	9 0	....	1230	....	....	3 15	3 45	....	....	....	5 53	6 40		....	8 30	....	....
—	1½ Humberstone ‡‡		7 9	....	9 4	....	1234	....	....	3 19	3 49	....	....	....	5 57	6 44		....	8 34	....	....
—	3¼ Thurnby and Scraptoft ...		7 17	....	9 9	....	1239	....	....	3 25	3 55	....	....	....	6 3	6 49		....	8 40	....	....
—	6½ Ingersby ††		7 26	....	9 16	....	1246	....	....	3 32	4 2	....	....	....	6 10	6 56		....	8 47	....	....
—	9¼ Lowesby		7 34	....	9 22	....	1253	....	....	3 39	4 8	....	....	....	6 21	7 1		....	8 54	....	....
16½	John O'Gaunt		7 42	8 18	9 27	10 34	1258	2 34	....	3 44	4 13	....	4 25	6 0	6 30	....		7 28	9 0	....	....
19½	Great Dalby		7 50	8 25	9 34	10 42	1 5	2 42	....	3 51	4 20	....	4 32	....	6 37	....		7 35	9 7	....	....
23¼	Melton Mowbray 590, 592 arr.		7 56	8 31	9 40	10 50	1 11	2 50	....	3 57	4 26	....	4 38	....	6 43	....		7 41	9 13	....	....
	Melton Mowbray dep.	7 30	8 2	8 34	9 42	10 53	1 15	2 53	....	3 59	4 28	....	4 41	....	6 46	....		7 44	....	....	....
26½	Scalford	7 40	8 11	8 41	9 48	11 0	1 23	3 0	....	4 5	4 34	....	4 48	....	6 55	....		7 51	....	....	....
28¼	Long Clawson and Hose	7 48	8 17	8 46	9 52	11 5	1 28	3 5	....	4 9	4 38	....	4 53	....	7 2	....		7 56	....	....	....
31	Harby and Stathern ..... arr.	7 56	8 22	8 53	9 58	11 12	1 34	3 11	....	4 15	4 44	....	4 58	....	7 7	....		8 2	....	....	....
—	Harby and Stathern .... dep.	8 6	....	8 55	....	11 14	....	3 14	....	Saturdays only.	Except Saturdays.	....	5 0	....	....	....		8 4		....	....
34½	Barnstone	8 20	....	9 3	....	11 22	....	3 22	....			....	5 8	....	....	....		8 12	Saturdays only.	....	....
38	Bingham Road †	8 32	....	9 11	....	11 30	....	3 30	....			....	5 16	....	....	....		....		....	....
41¼	Radcliffe-on-Trent 718, 721 arr.	....	....	9 17	....	11 36	....	3 36	....			....	5 22	....	....	....		8 25		....	....
	Radcliffe-on-Trent dep.	....	....	9 18	....	11 37	....	3 37	....			....	5 23	....	....	....		8 26		....	....
43½	Netherfield 711 ...... arr.	....	....	9 22	....	11 42	....	3 42	....			....	5 27	....	....	....		8 30		....	....
	Netherfield dep.	....	....	9 24	....	11 44	....	3 44	....			....	5 29	....	....	....		8 34		....	....
46	Nottingham * .... arr.	8 52	....	9 30	....	11 50	....	3 50	....			....	5 35	....	....	....		8 40		....	....
—	Harby and Stathern ...... dep.	....	8 29	....	10 0	....	1 37	....	....	4 16	4 46	....	....	....	7 13	....		....		....	....
34¾	Redmile, for Belvoir	....	8 37	....	10 6	....	1 45	....	....	4 22	4 52	....	....	....	7 22	....		....		....	....
41	Cotham	....	....	....	....	....	....	....	....	....	....	....	....	....	....	....		....	....	....	....
46½	Newark §§ 688, 600, 601 arr.	....	....	....	11b39	....	2b49	....	....	6b28	6b28	....	....	....	8b18	....		11b17	....	....	....
39¼	Bottesford	....	8 49	10d21	10 13	12d24	1 54	....	....	4 29	4 59	....	6d54	....	7 31	....		9d44	....	....	....
42½	Sedgebrook .... [736	....	8 56	10d28	....	12d31	2 1	....	....	4 36	5 6	....	7d1	....	....	....		....	....	....	....
46½	Grantham 688, 695, arr.	....	9 5	10d37	10 28	12d40	2 10	....	....	4 45	5 15	....	7d9	....	7 45	....		9d58	....	....	....
78½	736 Boston .... arr.	....	1035	12 7	12 7	3i17	4 44	....	....	7 40	7 40	....	....	....	10s0	....		8A58	....	....	....
103	736 Skegness .... "	....	1135	1 50	1 50	4i40	8 4	....	....	....	....	....	....	....	....	....		7A28	....	....	....
106½	736 Sutton-on-Sea .... "	....	1125	1 23	1 23	4H44	7 33	....	....	....	....	....	....	....	....	....		8B17	....	....	....
110½	736 Mablethorpe .... "	....	1132	1 30	1 30	4H51	7 40	....	....	....	....	....	....	....	....	....		8B9	....	....	....
151¾	695 London (K.C.) .... "	....	1130	1 5	1 5	3 50	5 0	....	....	7 10	8 47	....	9 25	....	10 0	....		3 25	....	....	....

A Except Sunday mornings; via Peterboro'.
b Via Grantham.
B Except Sunday mornings; via Peterboro' and Louth.
d Via Radcliffe-on-Trent.
H Via Peterboro'. Arrives Sutton-on-Sea at 5 2 and Mablethorpe at 5 9 aft. on Saturdays.
i Via Peterboro'.
s Saturdays only.
* London Road (Low Level).
† Over ¾ mile to Bingham Station.
†† Station for Houghton-on-the-Hill (1½ miles).
‡‡ ¼ mile to Humberstone Road Station.
§§ About 1 mile to L. M. & S. Station.

October 1923

	mrn	mrn	mrn	mrn	mrn	mrn	mrn	aft	aft	aft	aft	aft	aft	aft
Newark ..dep	5 25	5 25		9 15		1032	10 2			3 8			6 15	8 25
Cotham	**a**	**a**		**d**		1041	**a**						Sig.	
Red Mile *						1052				3 26			6 38	
Harby † ..arr				9 41		1058				3 32			6 44	
Grantham dp	7 35	8 0		9 23			1130	1215	2 58	2 58	3 20		6 12	
Sedgbrook							1138							
Bottesford	**b**	**b**		**b**			1146	1227	**b**	**b**			**b**	
Red Mile *	7 52	8 19		9 45			1153	1234	3 15				6 32	
Harby † ..arr		8 25		9 51			1159	1240	3 21	3 21			6 38	
Nottinghamd		8 0		9 23	1013		1130		3 0		3 55	6 0		
Netherfield **		8 6		9 29	1019		1136		3 6		4 1	6 6		
Radcliffe { ar		8 10			1023		1140				4 5	6 10		
Radcliffe { dp		8 11			1024		1141				4 8	6 11		
Binghm Road		8 26			1031		1148				4 13	6 18		
Barnstone		8 26			1036		1156				4 20	6 26		
Harby † ..arr		8 35		9 47	1044		12 5		3 27		4 28	6 33		
Harby †...dep	8 37		9 48	9 52	1045	1059	12 6	1241	3 28	3 33	4 32		6 35	6 45
Long Clawson	8 44			Sig.	1052		1218	1247			4 38		6 42	6 51
Scalford	8 48			10 1	1059		1218	1251			4 42		6 48	6 56
Melton { arr	8 9	8 55		10 7	11 5	1112	1224	1257	3 41	3 46	4 48		6 54	7 28 8 57
Mowbray { dep	8 10	8 57	9 10	10 9	1015	1114	1121	1226	1258	3 43	3 55	4 50	5 40	7 12 8 58
Great Dalby	8 17	9 5	9 17		1021	1121	1128	1233			4 24	4 58	5 47	7 17 26
Burrow ‡	8 23	9 13	9 23	1021	Sig.	1128	1135	1240	1 12		4 9	5 5	54	7 18 7 26
Loseby	8 29		9 29	Sig.				1 18		**f**		6 0		**e**
Ingersby §	8 36		9 36	Sig.		**e**		1 25		**ef**		6 7		**e**
Thurnby ¶	8 43		9 43	Sig.				1 32		**ef**		6 14		**e**
Humberstone	8 50		9 50	1048				1 39		**f**		6 21	7 43	
Leicester ‖ ar	8 54		9 54	1052		1155		1 43	4 30			6 25	7 47	9 28
Tilton		9 21			1136		1247				5 12		7 26	
East Norton		9 29			1144		1253				5 20		7 33	
Hallaton		9 35			1150		1259				5 26		7 39	
Market Har- { arr		9 46		1045	12 3		1 12		4 25		5 40		7 55	
bro' 178 { dep		9 57		1046	12 3		1 20		4 28		5 45	8 0		
Clipston & Oxenden		10 6			1211				4 36		5 54			
Kelmarsh		10 9			1214				4 39		5 57			
Lamport		1017			1222				4 48		7 5			
Brixworth		1023			1227				4 53		7 11			
Spratton		1026			1230				4 56		7 14			
Pitsford & Brampton		1031			1235				5 2		7 20			
Northampton(C.) ar		1040		1111	1243		1 50		5 12		7 30		8 25	

Vertical notes (top table): a Run via Grantham. b Stops when required to take up. c Stops when required to take up for Sheffield and Stations West thereof. d Stop when required to set down. o Via Radcliffe. e Stops to set down 1st class Passengers from Newark and Stations North thereof. f Stops on Tuesdays to set down from Melton.

Castle Station,	mrn	mrn	mrn	mrn	mrn	mrn	mrn	aft	aft	aft	aft	aft	aft	aft
Northampton ..dep		7 30		9 15		1048		1 0	2 30		4 50	6 0		
Pitsford & Brampton		7 39		9 24				1 9	2 39		4 59			
Spratton		7 45		9 30				1 15	2 45		5 5			
Brixworth		7 48		9 33				1 18	2 48		5 8			
Lamport		7 54		9 40				1 24	2 55		5 15			
Kelmarsh		8 2		9 49				1 32	3 3		5 22			
Clipston & Oxenden		8 5		9 54				1 36	3 7		5 26			
Market Har- { arr		8 15		10 4		1118		1 44	3 17		5 34	6 30		
bro' { dep		8 17		1010		1128		1 45	3 25			6 31	6 45	**c**
Hallaton		8 29		1022				1 57	3 37				6 57	
East Norton		8 34		1027				2 2	3 42				7 2	
Tilton	mrn	8 42		1034				2 10	3 49		aft		7 9	
Leicester ‖ dp	6 35	8 10		9 35		1040		1240	2 5		4 40	4 45		6 15
Humberstone		8 14		9 39				1244	**l**			4 49		6 19
Thurnby ¶		8 21		9 46		**h**		1251			**m**	4 56		6 26
Ingersby §		8 28		9 53		**h**		1258				5 3		6 33
Loseby		8 35		10 0				1 5				5 10		6 40
Burrow ‡		8 41	8 50	10 6	1041			1 11		2 17	3 56	5 16		7 16 6 46
Great Dalby		8 48	8 57	1013	1047			1 18		2 24	4 3	5 23		7 22 6 53
Melton { arr	7 5	8 55	9 4	1020	1053	1110	12 0	1 25	2 32	3 14	4 10	5 15	5 30	7 5 7 28
Mowbray { dep	7 6	7 15	9 6	1021	1055	1111	12 2	1 26	2 36		4 12	5 12		7 6 7 30
Scalford		7 26		1027	11 1		1 32			**f**	4 18			7 7 36
Long Clawson		7 36		1031	11 5		1 36				4 23			7 7 40
Harby † ..arr	**j**	7 43		9 21	1036	1111	1122	1214	1 42		2 48	4 28 5 24		7 19 7 14
Harby †..dep		7 46		9 22		1116		1215			2 50	4 32		7 20 7 47
Barnstone		7 57		9 29		1123					2 57	4 3		7 55
Binghm Road		8 7		9 37		1130					3 14	4 47		8 2
Radcliffe { ar		8 15		9 44		1137					3 21	4 54		8 12
Netherfield ** 146		3 22		9 52		1144		1234			3 27	5 1		7 39 8 18
Nottinghama		8 30		9 58		1150		1240			3 33	5 7		7 45 8 25
Harby †..dep				9 30	1037			1 43			2 50	5 30		
Red Mile *				9 36	1043			1 49				**d**		
Bottesford				9 43	1050			1 56				**d**		
Sedgbrok[143]				**dk**	1057			2 3						
Grantham153				9 55	11 6	1228		2 12		3 13	5g32	5g32		
Harby †..dep	**j**				1123	1219		1 43	**a**	**a**	5 25		7 15
Red Mile *					1129	1225		1 49			5 31		7 21
Cotham .[235]					1141			1 56					**d**
Newark 140, ar	7 40		11 0		1150	1245	2 48	4 10		5 50			7 40

Vertical notes (lower table): h Stops to take up 1st class Passengers for Newark and Stations North thereof. j Stops to take up 1st class Passengers for Newark and Stations North thereof. d Stops to set down 1st class Passengers from Leicester. k Stops when required to take up for Newark. l Stops to take up for London. m Stops to take up for Grantham and Stations North thereof. n Stops to take up for Newark and Stations North thereof.

June 1883

July 1960

Table 231 — LEICESTER, MELTON MOWBRAY NORTH, SKEGNESS and MABLETHORPE

Miles		Week Days			Sundays		Miles		Week Days			Sundays	
		am	am	..	am	..			pm	pm	..	pm	..
	Leicester (Belgrave Rd.) dep	8 25	9 10	..	9 45	..		Mablethorpe ...dep		1 52	..	..	..
1¾	Humberstone	8 32	9 17	..	9 51	..	2¼	Sutton-on-Sea ,,		2 0	..	..	..
3¼	Thurnby & Scraptoft	8 38	9 23	..	9 57	..	30¼	Skegness ,,	1 20		..	7 26	..
18¼	MeltonMowbrayNorth { arr	9 6	9 52	..	1024	..	30¾	Boston ,,	1 58	2 45	..		..
	{ dep	9 8	9 56	..	1028	..	69¼	Bottesford ...dep		3 48	..		..
33	Bottesford ...arr		1026	..		..	84¼	MeltonMowbrayNorth { arr	3 28	4 16	..	9 27	..
72¼	Boston ...arr	1035	1130	..		..		{ dep	3 32	4 20	..	9 32	..
96½	Skegness ,,	1117	1239	..	1228	..	99¼	Thurnby & Scraptoft	4 4	4 52	..	10 0	..
100	Sutton-on-Sea ,,	1141	1224	..		..	101¼	Humberstone	4 9	4 57	..	10 7	..
102¾	Mablethorpe ,,	1149	1232	..		..	102¾	Leicester (Belgrave Rd.) arr	4 14	5 2	..	1012	..

(Week Days columns: "Saturdays only" / "Saturdays only"; Sundays columns shown as note)

114.   A local train is seen on 28th April 1956 behind no. 64235, another J6. It is suffering an overheated smokebox door. This was in the era of workmens trains, twice on weekdays. By 1953, there had been only one public train in and out on weekdays; 8.17am and 6.10pm. It served Melton Mowbray. (T.G.Hepburn/M.J.Stretton)

115.   No. 158A was on display in June 1957 as part of the show for the centenary of the MR's arrival in Leicester from Hitchin. It was a 2-4-0 of a type used on early passenger trains. (Milepost 92½)

116.   One can imagine the impressive echo that was to be enjoyed by the two onlookers on 5th September 1959, as class B1 4-6-0 no. 61177 rumbled in from the East Coast. The van could be used for excess luggage and prams. (P.J.Shoesmith)

117.   Seen on the same day, is no. 61177 again. The clock shows 5.5 and so it must be the 1.52pm from Mablethorpe. The sunlight is enhancing the atmosphere. (P.J.Shoesmith)

118.   This 50-lever box was for long known as No.1 Box and is seen on 20th June 1961. Its closure came on 20th January 1968. The cattle dock behind had become part of Vic Berry's scrapyard. (B.Hilton/M.J.Stretton)

0068 **2nd-SINGLE   SINGLE-2nd** **0068**
Leicester (Belgrave Road) to
Leicester   Leicester
(Belgrave Road)   (Belgrave Road)
Sutton-on-Sea   Sutton-on-Sea
SUTTON-ON-SEA
via Melton Mowbray, Bottesford & Boston
(M)   20/3   Fare   20/3   (M)
For conditions see over   For conditions se. over

4186 L . N . E . R . **4186**
not transferable. This ticket is Issued subject to th
General Notices, Regulations & Conditions in the Co'
current Time Tables. Available on day of issue only
HUMBERSTONE to
SKEGNESS
Via Redmile Grantham & Boston
Fare /   S   \   11s.1d.
THIRD / 351 \ CLASS
SKEGNESS

119.   Running in from Mablethorpe on 29th July 1961 is class B1 no. 61209 and we can enjoy the fine array of starting signals - one for each platform. All would be redundant in about 15 months, but would remain in place until the end. (D.Richards/M.J.Stretton)

120.   This panorama is from 20th June 1964 and is included to show the massive goods shed. Such traffic ceased on 14th December 1964. The tankers served a petrol depot on the other side of Catherine Street bridge. The goods yard once had a 10-ton crane. (E.Wilmshurst)

MP Middleton Press

EVOLVING THE ULTIMATE RAIL ENCYCLOPEDIA

Easebourne Lane, Midhurst, West Sussex.
GU29 9AZ Tel:01730 813169

www.middletonpress.co.uk email:info@middletonpress.co.uk

A-978 0 906520 B- 978 1 873793 C- 978 1 901706 D-978 1 904474
E - 978 1 906008 F - 978 1 908174

All titles listed below were in print at time of publication - please check current availability by looking at our website - *www.middletonpress.co.uk* or by requesting a Brochure which includes our *LATEST* RAILWAY TITLES also our TRAMWAY, TROLLEYBUS, MILITARY and COASTAL series

A
Abergavenny to Merthyr C 91 8
Abertillery & Ebbw Vale Lines D 84 5
Aberystwyth to Carmarthen E 90 1
Allhallows - Branch Line to A 62 8
Alton - Branch Lines to A 11 6
Andover to Southampton A 82 6
Ascot - Branch Lines around A 64 2
Ashburton - Branch Line to B 95 4
Ashford - Steam to Eurostar B 67 1
Ashford to Dover A 48 2
Austrian Narrow Gauge D 04 3
Avonmouth - BL around D 42 5
Aylesbury to Rugby D 91 3

B
Baker Street to Uxbridge D 90 6
Bala to Llandudno E 87 1
Banbury to Birmingham D 27 2
Banbury to Cheltenham E 63 5
Bangor to Holyhead F 01 7
Bangor to Portmadoc E 72 7
Barking to Southend C 80 2
Barmouth to Pwllheli E 53 6
Barry - Branch Lines around D 50 0
Bartlow - Branch Lines to F 27 7
Bath Green Park to Bristol C 36 9
Bath to Evercreech Junction A 60 4
Beamish 40 years on rails E94 9
Bedford to Wellingborough D 31 9
Berwick to Drem F 64 2
Berwick to St. Boswells F 75 8
B'ham to Tamworth & Nuneaton F 63 5
Birkenhead to West Kirby F 61 1
Birmingham to Wolverhampton E253
Bletchley to Cambridge D 94 4
Bletchley to Rugby E 07 9
Bodmin - Branch Lines around B 83 1
Boston to Lincoln F 80 2
Bournemouth to Evercreech Jn A 46 8
Bournemouth to Weymouth A 57 4
Bradshaw's History F18 5
Bradshaw's Rail Times 1850 F 13 0
Bradshaw's Rail Times 1895 F 11 6
Branch Lines series - see town names
Brecon to Neath D 43 2
Brecon to Newport D 16 6
Brecon to Newtown E 06 2
Brighton to Eastbourne A 16 1
Brighton to Worthing A 03 1
Bristol to Taunton D 03 6
Bromley South to Rochester B 23 7
Bromsgrove to Birmingham D 87 6
Bromsgrove to Gloucester D 73 9
Broxbourne to Cambridge F16 1
Brunel - A railtour D 74 6
Bude - Branch Line to B 29 9
Burnham to Evercreech Jn B 68 0

C
Cambridge to Ely D 55 5
Canterbury - BLs around B 58 9
Cardiff to Dowlais (Cae Harris) E 47 5
Cardiff to Pontypridd E 95 6
Cardiff to Swansea E 42 0
Carlisle to Hawick E 85 7
Carmarthen to Fishguard E 66 6
Caterham & Tattenham Corner B251
Central & Southern Spain NG E 91 8
Chard and Yeovil - BLs a C 30 7
Charing Cross to Dartford A 75 8
Charing Cross to Orpington A 96 3
Cheddar - Branch Line to B 90 9
Cheltenham to Andover C 43 7
Cheltenham to Redditch D 81 4
Chester to Birkenhead F 21 5
Chester to Manchester F 51 2
Chester to Rhyl E 93 2
Chester to Warrington F 40 6
Chichester to Portsmouth A 14 7
Clacton and Walton - BLs to F 04 8
Clapham Jn to Beckenham Jn B 36 7
Cleobury Mortimer - BLs a E 18 5
Clevedon & Portishead - BLs to D180
Consett to South Shields E 57 4
Cornwall Narrow Gauge D 56 2
Corris and Vale of Rheidol E 65 9
Craven Arms to Llandeilo E 35 2
Craven Arms to Wellington E 33 8
Crawley to Littlehampton A 34 5
Crewe to Manchester F 57 4
Cromer - Branch Lines around C 26 0
Croydon to East Grinstead B 48 0
Crystal Palace & Catford Loop B 87 1
Cyprus Narrow Gauge E 13 0

D
Darjeeling Revisited F 09 3
Darlington Leamside Newcastle E 28 4
Darlington to Newcastle D 98 2
Dartford to Sittingbourne B 34 3
Denbigh - Branch Lines around F 32 1
Derwent Valley - BL to the D 06 7
Devon Narrow Gauge E 09 3
Didcot to Banbury D 02 9
Didcot to Swindon C 84 0
Didcot to Winchester C 13 0
Dorset & Somerset NG D 76 0
Douglas - Laxey - Ramsey E 75 8
Douglas to Peel C 88 8
Douglas to Port Erin C 55 0
Douglas to Ramsey D 39 5
Dover to Ramsgate A 78 9
Dublin Northwards in 1950s E 31 4
Dunstable - Branch Lines to E 27 7

E
Ealing to Slough C 42 0
Eastbourne to Hastings A 27 7
East Cornwall Mineral Railways D 22 7
East Croydon to Three Bridges A 53 6
Eastern Spain Narrow Gauge E 56 7
East Grinstead - BLs to A 07 9
East London - Branch Lines of C 44 4
East London Line B 80 0
East of Norwich - Branch Lines E 69 7
Effingham Junction - BLs a A 74 1
Ely to Norwich C 90 1
Enfield Town & Palace Gates D 32 6
Epsom to Horsham A 30 7
Eritrean Narrow Gauge E 38 3
Euston to Harrow & Wealdstone C 89 5
Exeter to Barnstaple B 15 2
Exeter to Newton Abbot C 49 9
Exeter to Tavistock B 69 5
Exmouth - Branch Lines to B 00 8

F
Fairford - Branch Line to A 52 9
Falmouth, Helston & St. Ives C 74 1
Fareham to Salisbury A 67 3
Faversham to Dover B 05 3
Felixstowe & Aldeburgh - BL to D 20 3
Fenchurch Street to Barking C 20 8
Festiniog - 50 yrs of enterprise C 83 3
Festiniog 1946-55 E 01 7
Festiniog in the Fifties B 68 8
Festiniog in the Sixties B 91 6
Ffestiniog in Colour 1955-82 F 25 3
Finsbury Park to Alexandra Pal C 02 8
Frome to Bristol B 77 0

G
Galashiels to Edinburgh F 52 9
Gloucester to Bristol D 35 7
Gloucester to Cardiff D 66 1
Gosport - Branch Lines around A 36 9
Greece Narrow Gauge D 72 2

H
Hampshire Narrow Gauge D 36 4
Harrow to Watford D 14 2
Harwich & Hadleigh - BLs to F 02 4
Harz Revisited F 62 8
Hastings to Ashford A 37 6
Hawick to Galashiels F 36 9
Hawkhurst - Branch Line to A 66 6
Hayling - Branch Line to A 12 3
Hay-on-Wye - BL around D 92 0
Haywards Heath to Seaford A 28 4
Hemel Hempstead - BLs to D 88 3
Henley, Windsor & Marlow - BLa C77 2
Hereford to Newport D 54 8
Hertford & Hatfield - BLs a E 58 1
Hertford Loop E 71 0
Hexham to Carlisle D 75 3
Hexham to Hawick F 08 6
Hitchin to Peterborough D 07 4
Holborn Viaduct to Lewisham A 81 9
Horsham - Branch Lines to A 02 4
Huntingdon - Branch Line to A 93 2

I
Ilford to Shenfield C 97 0
Ilfracombe - Branch Line to B 21 3
Industrial Rlys of the South East A 09 3
Ipswich to Saxmundham C 41 3
Isle of Wight Lines - 50 yrs C 12 3
Italy Narrow Gauge F 17 8

K
Kent Narrow Gauge C 45 1
Kidderminster to Shrewsbury E 10 9
Kingsbridge - Branch Line to C 98 7
Kings Cross to Potters Bar E 62 8
King's Lynn to Hunstanton F 58 1
Kingston & Hounslow Loops A 83 3
Kingswear - Branch Line to C 17 8

L
Lambourn - Branch Line to C 70 3
Launceston & Princetown - BLs C 19 2
Lewisham to Dartford A 92 5
Lincoln to Cleethorpes F 56 7
Lines around Wimbledon B 75 6
Liverpool Street to Chingford D 01 2
Liverpool Street to Ilford C 34 5
Llandeilo to Swansea E 46 8
London Bridge to Addiscombe B 20 6
London Bridge to East Croydon A 58 1
Longmoor - Branch Lines to A 41 3
Looe - Branch Line to C 22 2
Loughborough to Nottingham F 68 0
Lowestoft - BLs around E 40 6
Ludlow to Hereford E 14 7
Lydney - Branch Lines around E 26 0
Lyme Regis - Branch Line to A 45 1
Lynton - Branch Line to B 04 6

M
Machynlleth to Barmouth E 54 3
Maesteg and Tondu Lines E 06 2
Majorca & Corsica Narrow Gauge F 41 3
March - Branch Lines around B 09 1
Market Drayton - BLs around F 67 3
Marylebone to Rickmansworth D 49 4
Melton Constable to Yarmouth Bch E031
Midhurst - Branch Lines of E 78 9
Midhurst - Branch Lines to F 00 0
Minehead - Branch Line to A 80 2
Mitcham Junction Lines B 01 5
Monmouth - Branch Lines to E 20 8
Monmouthshire Eastern Valleys D 71 5
Moretonhampstead - BL to C 27 7
Moreton-in-Marsh to Worcester D 26 5
Mountain Ash to Neath D 80 7

N
Newark to Doncaster F 78 9
Newbury to Westbury C 66 6
Newcastle to Hexham D 69 2
Newport (IOW) - Branch Lines to A 26 0
Newquay - Branch Lines to C 71 0
Newton Abbot to Plymouth C 60 4
Newtown to Aberystwyth E 41 3
North East German NG D 44 9
Northern Alpine Narrow Gauge F 37 6
Northern France Narrow Gauge C 75 8
Northern Spain Narrow Gauge E 83 3
North London Line B 94 7
North of Birmingham F 55 0
North Woolwich - BLs around C 65 9
Nottingham to Boston F 70 3
Nottingham to Lincoln F 43 7

O
Ongar - Branch Line to E 05 5
Orpington to Tonbridge B 03 9
Oswestry - Branch Lines around E 60 4
Oswestry to Whitchurch E 81 9
Oxford to Bletchley D 57 9
Oxford to Moreton-in-Marsh D 15 9

P
Paddington to Ealing C 37 6
Paddington to Princes Risborough C819
Padstow - Branch Line to B 54 1
Pembroke and Cardigan - BLs to F 29 1
Peterborough to Kings Lynn E 32 1
Peterborough to Newark F 72 7
Plymouth - BLs around B 98 5
Plymouth to St. Austell C 63 5
Pontypool to Mountain Ash D 65 4
Pontypridd to Merthyr F 14 7
Pontypridd to Port Talbot E 86 4
Porthmadog 1954-94 - BLa B 31 2
Portmadoc 1923-46 - BLa B 13 8
Portsmouth to Southampton A 31 4
Portugal Narrow Gauge E 67 3
Potters Bar to Cambridge D 70 8
Princes Risborough - BL to D 05 0
Princes Risborough to Banbury C 85 7

R
Railways to Victory C 16 1
Reading to Basingstoke B 27 5
Reading to Didcot C 79 6
Reading to Guildford A 47 5
Redhill to Ashford A 73 4
Return to Blaenau 1970-82 C 64 2
Rhyl to Bangor F 15 4
Rhymney & New Tredegar Lines E 48 2
Rickmansworth to Aylesbury D 61 6
Romania & Bulgaria NG E 23 9
Romneyrail C 32 1
Ross-on-Wye - BLs around E 30 7
Ruabon to Barmouth E 84 0
Rugby to Birmingham E 37 6
Rugby to Loughborough F 12 3
Rugby to Stafford F 07 9
Ryde to Ventnor A 19 2

S
Salisbury to Westbury B 39 8
Sardinia and Sicily Narrow Gauge F 50 5
Saxmundham to Yarmouth C 69 7
Saxony & Baltic Germany Revisited F 71 0
Saxony Narrow Gauge D 47 0
Seaton & Sidmouth - BLs to A 95 6
Selsey - Branch Line to A 04 8
Sheerness - Branch Line to B 16 2
Shenfield to Ipswich E 96 3
Shrewsbury - Branch Line to A 86 4
Shrewsbury to Chester E 70 3
Shrewsbury to Crewe F 48 2
Shrewsbury to Ludlow E 21 5
Shrewsbury to Newtown E 29 1
Sierra Leone Narrow Gauge D 28 9
Sirhowy Valley Line E 12 3
Sittingbourne to Ramsgate A 90 1
Slough to Newbury C 56 7
South African Two-foot gauge E 51 2
Southampton to Bournemouth A 42 0
Southend & Southminster BLs E 76 5
Southern Alpine Narrow Gauge F 22 2
Southern France Narrow Gauge C 47 5
South London Line B 46 6
South Lynn to Norwich City F 03 1
Southwold - Branch Line to A 15 4
Spalding - Branch Lines around E 52 9
Spalding to Grimsby F 65 9 6
Stafford to Chester F 34 5
Stafford to Wellington F 59 8
St Albans to Bedford D 08 1
St. Austell to Penzance C 67 3
St. Boswell to Berwick F 44 4
Steaming Through Isle of Wight A
Steaming Through West Hants A
Stourbridge to Wolverhampton E
St. Pancras to Barking D 68 5
St. Pancras to Folkestone E 88 8
St. Pancras to St. Albans C 78 9
Stratford to Cheshunt F 53 6
Stratford-u-Avon to Birmingham
Stratford-u-Avon to Cheltenham
Sudbury - Branch Lines to F 19 2
Surrey Narrow Gauge C 87 1
Sussex Narrow Gauge C 68 0
Swanley to Ashford B 45 9
Swansea - Branch Lines around
Swansea to Carmarthen E 59 8
Swindon to Bristol C 96 3
Swindon to Gloucester D 46 3
Swindon to Newport D 30 2
Swiss Narrow Gauge C 94 9

T
Talyllyn 60 E 98 7
Tamworth to Derby F 76 5
Taunton to Barnstaple B 60 2
Taunton to Exeter C 82 6
Taunton to Minehead F 39 0
Tavistock to Plymouth B 88 6
Tenterden - Branch Line to A 21
Three Bridges to Brighton A 35 2
Tilbury Loop C 86 4
Tiverton - BLs around C 62 8
Tivetshall to Beccles D 41 8
Tonbridge to Hastings A 44 4
Torrington - Branch Lines to B 37
Towcester - BLs around E 39 0
Tunbridge Wells BLs A 32 1

U
Upwell - Branch Line to B 64 0

V
Victoria to Bromley South A 98 7
Victoria to East Croydon A 40 6
Vivarais Revisited E 08 6

W
Walsall Routes F 45 1
Wantage - Branch Line to D 25 8
Wareham to Swanage 50 yrs D0
Waterloo to Windsor A 54 3
Waterloo to Woking A 38 3
Watford to Leighton Buzzard D 45
Wellingborough to Leicester F 73
Welshpool to Llanfair E 49 9
Wenford Bridge to Fowey C 09 3
Westbury to Bath B 55 8
Westbury to Taunton C 76 5
West Cornwall Mineral Rlys D 48
West Croydon to Epsom B 08 4
West German Narrow Gauge D 9
West London - BLs of C 50 5
West London Line B 84 8
West Wiltshire - BLs of D 12 8
Weymouth - BLs A 65 9
Willesden Jn to Richmond B 71 8
Wimbledon to Beckenham C 58 1
Wimbledon to Epsom B 62 6
Wimborne - BLs around A 97 0
Wisbech - BLs around C 01 7
Witham & Kelvedon - BLs a E 82
Woking to Alton A 59 8
Woking to Portsmouth A 25 3
Woking to Southampton A 55 0
Wolverhampton to Shrewsbury E
Wolverhampton to Stafford F 79 6
Worcester to Birmingham D 97 5
Worcester to Hereford D 38 8
Worthing to Chichester A 06 2
Wrexham to New Brighton F 47 5
Wroxham - BLs around F 31 4

Y
Yeovil - 50 yrs change C 38 3
Yeovil to Dorchester A 76 5
Yeovil to Exeter A 91 8
York to Scarborough F 23 9